THE
SMITH
MANOEUVRE

Is your mortgage tax deductible?

Fraser Smith

Outspan Publishing

THE SMITH MANOEUVRE

by
Fraser Smith

Sixth Printing – January 2006

Copyright © 2002 by
Fraser Smith

Outspan Publishing
201-9800 McDonald Park Road
Sidney, BC   V8L 5W5

National Library of Canada Cataloguing in Publication Data

Smith, Fraser, 1938-

The Smith manoeuvre / Fraser Smith

ISBN 0-9732952-0-1

1. Mortgage loans--Canada
2. Income tax deductions for interest--Canada. I. Title.
HG2040.5C2S62 2002   336.24'216   C2002-904141-4

Cover Design by Art Department Design,
Victoria, British Columbia, Canada
www.artdepartmentdesign.com

Printed and Produced in Canada by:
Centax Books/Publishing Solutions,
a Division of PrintWest Communications Ltd.
1150 Eighth Avenue, Regina, Saskatchewan, Canada S4R 1C9
Telephone (306) 525-2304   Fax: (306) 757-2439
www.centaxbooks.com   centax@printwest.com

To my wife Judy
and our wonderful
family. They make
the work worthwhile.

ACKNOWLEGEMENTS

I owe a great debt of gratitude to my family and friends who have encouraged me to push ahead with this book, and I thank them for their interest and support.

Until you try to write a book, you do not comprehend in the slightest what it takes in the way of technical and professional assistance to make it happen. I certainly have that understanding now, and I wish to express my appreciation to all those people who helped me with my creation.

Special thanks to special people are in order beginning with Larry Bell the former C.E.O. of VanCity Savings Credit Union who saw something others had missed. Thank you to Tom Hancock and his peers and staff at VanCity who have been part of this for over two decades now. Thanks to Preston Manning, Elizabeth Nickson, Herb Grubel and Moshe Milevsky for their encouragement.

The book, the software and the website (_www.smithman.net_) (never miss a chance) happened because of first rank professionals doing their magic on my behalf. They are Bruce Batchelor president of Trafford Publishing and Jennifer Taylor my Special Agent. The covers of this book were created by my ace designer, Victor Crapnell. Spreadsheet translation was by my favourite engineer with the iron ring, Carol Maas. The Visual Basic programming and website design is the excellent work of the Dynamic Duo, Norman Sim and Ken De'Ath. Oscar Gomez is the talented software writer who has re-programmed The Smithman Calculator in Java.

Many people supplied ideas, insight, encouragement and editing skills. They are Gordon and Mary Jane Shaw, Frank Edgell, Tom Bazin, John Schreiner, Bob Baillie, Brian Dougherty, C.A., Paul Winstanby, C.A., Troy Lanigan, Eric and Jennifer Verscheure and Rob Smith, M.B.A. My thanks to them all.

This book would not likely have been written but for the patience, dedication, loyalty and long and extra hours put in by my long-time assistant and good friend, LuAnn Olson. It's LuAnn who really runs this place, and I'm grateful.

Lastly, I'd like to recognize all those dedicated, hard working Canadian families doing their part to keep Canada a great place to live. It is a privilege to be able to pass on to those families with house mortgages the means to improve their wealth utilizing The Smith Manoeuvre.

Fraser Smith
Sidney, B.C.   July 2005

FOREWORD

In 1984, the Board of Directors of Vancouver City Savings determined to take steps to secure their dominant position in the British Columbia and Canadian credit union movement.

As Chief Executive Officer at the time, I felt it was propitious that Fraser Smith had targeted VanCity to champion his unique financial strategy for mortgage owners in Canada. The Smith Manoeuvre, as it was to become known, was simple and elegant. We attracted many new customers over the years by virtue of our support of the program.

My question back then still stands today – "Why isn't every Canadian making his mortgage tax deductible?" Perhaps the publishing of "The Smith Manoeuvre" will make it happen.

Larry Bell, Chair
B.C. Hydro
Vancouver, B.C.

DISCLAIMER

The information contained in this book has been developed over several years of experience and is believed to be accurate and reliable. The reader is reminded that there may be variations in the interpretation of various laws and regulations in different jurisdictions because of the nature of the subject matter being dealt with.

The author and publisher specifically disclaim any liability arising from loss, personal or otherwise, incurred directly or indirectly as a consequence of the use and application of any of the information contained in this book. In no event will the author, publisher, or any distributor of this book be liable to the purchaser for any amount greater than the purchase price of this book.

This publication is sold with the understanding that neither the author nor the publisher is engaged in rendering legal, financial planning, investment, accounting, tax, or other professional assistance or advice. If legal, investment, financial planning, accounting, tax, or other professional assistance or advice is required, you should seek the services of a competent professional with the required qualifications.

CONTENTS

INTRODUCTION

On the average, the financial life of the average Canadian is, well, average. But you can't trust averages. When you are sitting on a block of ice with a bare ass, and your hair is on fire, on the average, you feel good.

If you have read this far, and are starting to realize that The Smith Manoeuvre is not the title of Robert Ludlum's latest novel, do not despair. Sometimes, real-life is more interesting than fiction.

Today you are going to learn how to re-engineer the way you deal with your house mortgage. When you implement the strategy you are about to discover, it will cause the taxman to send you tax refund cheques, big ones, each year until you die at age 130. The tax refund cheques come every year, they are free, there is no tax on them and it is all perfectly legal.

These are not small tax refunds. Your mortgage payments for a year total a huge number. As much as 70% or 80% of that huge number is the interest you are paying the bank. 80% of a huge number is also a huge number. Let's say it's $10,000 for our Mr. Joe Average. Joe likes tax deductions. Every year he buys a $10,000 RRSP. (He has to first earn an extra $20,000 for the year so he can give up half to all the governments who want all their taxes, leaving him $10,000 to buy his RRSP). So Joe buys his $10,000 RRSP and claims a $10,000 tax deduction when he submits his income tax return. A few weeks later, Joe gets a lovely cheque from the taxman for $4,000 being 40% of the tax deduction he claimed. That's a 40% return on his "investment" which is excellent performance.

What Joe doesn't know is that hidden in his annual mortgage payments is another $10,000 tax deduction, which is free for the arranging. And he doesn't have to go and earn another $20,000 before tax to get it. If he reads this book, he will learn how easy and inexpensive it is to convert an expense he is already paying, his mortgage interest, into a tax deduction that will yield equivalent benefits to what he would receive if he bought an RRSP. Not only that, once the conversion has been effected, the tax deductions will be automatic and free every year for as many years into the future as he still has the loan.

If you have a mortgage you could have the same advantages as Joe Average.

But that's not all. Simultaneously you will begin now to build an investment portfolio of your own choosing. You will decide whether you want to invest in stocks, bonds, mutual funds, investment real estate, your own business or somebody else's business. These investments will be free and clear.

It sounds too good to be true. But before you adopt that assumption, consider that The Smith Manoeuvre has been operating continuously since 1984, tax lawyers from several of Canada's top law firms have confirmed to several large financial institutions that this is a creative but legal financial strategy. Revenue Canada auditors have interviewed me and my Manoeuvre in my office and thousands of people are enjoying the luxury of The Smith Manoeuvre with more being added every month.

Len and Clarence Bick are co-founders of venerable Bick Financial Security Corporation in beautiful Ancaster, Ontario. With 15 financial planners and a half billion in assets under administration, Len is what you would recognize as a savvy businessman. Last year he was quoted as saying, "The Smith Manoeuvre is like a small snowball just starting to roll down a hill covered in wet snow. This exciting new financial strategy will give every Canadian family with a mortgage the chance to make their debt tax deductible. Big things are going to start happening in the financial planning and investment industries."

You may well ask, "Why isn't every Canadian doing this?" The answer is that I haven't met them all yet. The next best thing was to write this book, explain how it works and how to arrange these free benefits for your family. It's my gift to Canadians. I take great pleasure in the knowledge that many who read this book will be empowered to substantially improve the financial life of their family utilizing these tools of the wealthy. A little knowledge is a magnificent thing in the hands of the motivated. So do order the software (see the last page of this book) so you can run various versions of your own numbers and circumstances. Then, go to a financial planner and ask him or her to confirm the validity of the assumptions and projections. Then retain him or her to implement The Smith Manoeuvre for you. You will be glad you did.

Fraser Smith
Sidney, B.C.
July 2005

1

IN A NUTSHELL

What is The Smith Manoeuvre?

The Smith Manoeuvre is a creative, legal financial strategy that will generate free annual tax refunds for many years into the future for any Canadian who has a house mortgage. Your mortgage will melt away as fast as your investment portfolio grows. The wealthy class has used this strategy for years, with the blessing of the taxman. This book extends the knowledge and provides instructions to all the rest of us. It will make a huge positive impact on your family's net worth.

The Smith Manoeuvre converts non-deductible interest debt (bad debt) to tax-deductible-interest debt (good debt). Bad-debt loans such as car loans, vacation loans and especially home mortgage loans cost Canadians huge amounts of non-deductible interest every year. If this same amount of interest was a tax deduction, impressive tax refund cheques would start appearing as free gifts from the taxman each year.

If you have interest to pay anyway, why not at least convert it to interest that gives you generous, free, gratis, no charge, tax paid gifts each year? This gift will be courtesy of the Canada Revenue Agency (CRA) (formerly known as Revenue Canada). They will be quite happy to send you a big, juicy refund cheque every year until you die at age 130.

You only need to take the time to reorganize the structure of the debt you are already carrying. Then the tax refund cheques start coming. Free. No charge. Gifts.

Just How Large Will These Cheques from the Taxman Be?

The interest on a new $100,000 mortgage at 7% would be $6,852 in interest expense in the first year, non-deductible. If this mortgage was a tax-deductible mortgage, and if you were at the 40% tax bracket, you would receive a cheque from the taxman for $6,852 x .40 = $2,740 as a gift.

If your mortgage were $200,000 at 7%, your free gift from the CRA would be double at $5,481. Free. No tax to pay on the gift either. It is truly free, no strings attached. Deductible interest is far better than non-deductible interest.

There is Another Large Advantage

If you are a Canadian using The Smith Manoeuvre, in addition to the gift of generous tax refunds, you will meet another objective common to all of us. You will become the owner of a portfolio of assets such as stocks, bonds, mutual funds and investment real estate. You could invest in your own business, or someone else's business. You will choose the investments. The assets will be free and clear – they will be unencumbered. There will be no margin calls. The purchase of these new assets will begin *now*, the generation of tax deductions will begin *now*, and the non-deductible debt will begin to disappear *now*.

The free tax refund cheques are great, and to see that ugly mortgage melt away before your eyes is superb. But the integrated benefit of a free and clear investment portfolio growing rapidly in your hands is truly magnificent.

Karl Ruban is a financial planner with Assante in Ontario. He is an ardent supporter of The Smith Manoeuvre and is also well trained for his profession. He has an Honours B. Comm., he is a Chartered Accountant, a Certified Management Accountant, A Chartered Financial Planner and a Registered Financial Planner. He commutes between his offices in Toronto and Ottawa.

Karl read this book on the train in 2003 and subsequently has helped dozens of families implement The Smith Manoeuvre. His point with his clients is that the investment portfolio is really their personal, private, unregistered pension plan. The doubts that abound regarding corporate and government pension plans are less worrisome when you have built a pension plan that you control. Take it from Karl.

Are There Any Rules?

In Canada, when you borrow to buy a car, to go on a vacation, to consolidate your consumer loans or to buy your home, you are prevented by law from claiming the annual interest expense of these loans as a tax deduction. Americans generally can deduct this interest at tax time, and accordingly they pay less tax than we Canadians. This is a major factor when trying to figure out why an American lives to such a higher standard than his Canadian counterpart.

Sounds like we are doomed. But just a minute. One type of interest in Canada *is* tax deductible. If the money you borrow is for the purpose of investing, where you expect to earn income, then the interest on *that* loan *is* deductible.

Remember this - the test for deductibility of interest is: *What did you do with the money when you borrowed it?* Bought a car? Forget it. Bought a home? No dice. The loan interest in these examples is *not* deductible because the purpose of the borrowing was *not* to invest, it was for consumption.

So we have a problem. You already own a house with a mortgage, which is not deductible. Most of my clients come to me carrying perhaps the largest debt they will own in their lifetime, their mortgage, and it's non-deductible.

You already have the bad-debt mortgage - is it too late for you?

Not if you know how to utilize The Smith Manoeuvre.

What Should You Do?

You already have the mortgage loan, or the car loan, or maybe a consumer loan or line of credit, maybe credit card debt - all non-deductible interest loans. You would also be glad to be building an investment portfolio if you could, but you feel you need to get your debt paid off first.

Your plan is to get the debt down over the next few years, and then you expect to be able to start an investment program. This is a significant recommendation for Canadians made by Garth Turner, one of Canada's pre-eminent financial gurus. His excellent book *The Strategy* is a must read for Canadians serious about their financial well-being.

Most of the financial planning books tell you to do it that way. Pay off your mortgage, and then start an investment program. Your friends, family, neighbours and work mates are all doing it that way, so it must be right. But it's not.

There is a much better way. Organize your financial life to set up The Smith Manoeuvre.

Step 1   Read this book

Step 2   Order The Smithman Calculator so that you can do calculations based on your own financial circumstances (see the last page of this book for ordering instructions, or go to *www.smithman.net*).

Step 3   Ask your financial planner to organize The Smith Manoeuvre for you.

Step 4   If you don't have a financial planner, think seriously about getting one. Find one who implements The Smith Manoeuvre for his or her clients.

Summary

Most Canadians would like:
1. To get rid of their house mortgage as soon as possible.
2. To own lots of investments to ensure a financially successful retirement.

Most Canadians attack these two wishes sequentially, and many financial planners encourage them to do so – pay off their mortgage, then start an investment program.

What's wrong with that?

It is better than doing nothing, but to take 15 or 20 years of your life to deal with the mortgage before you begin to invest will lose you 15 or 20 years of compounding time in your investment portfolio.

The Smith Manoeuvre has you getting rid of your old mortgage very quickly while *simultaneously* starting your lifelong investment program – *now*. We can accomplish these two objectives at the same time, starting *now*. Wealth creation takes time. The Smith Manoeuvre gives you the gift of all the time you have remaining for the rest of your life, to build your wealth while getting rid of that bad-debt mortgage - simultaneously.

In addition, free, new money from the taxman begins to be generated *now*. *Now* is very important. It matters not how old you are, how wealthy you are or whether you're a socialist or a free-enterpriser. The bad news is that you have the wrong kind of debt, and it's killing you slowly. The good news is that it is easy to fix.

Take action *now*. Remember that old saying, "Today is the first day of the rest of your financial life." You can optimize your financial future by engaging the power of The Smith Manoeuvre. Do it *now*.

2

IN THE BEGINNING

It all began in Vancouver

In 1980, long before it was fashionable, my wife Judy and I went in for financial planning. Like the Remington shaver guy, Victor Kiam, "I liked it so much I joined the company" and I apprenticed the personal financial planning business. In 1981, with four great friends and partners, Granville West was founded in Vancouver, and we never looked back. Granville West has become a powerful Vancouver corporate entity specializing in financial planning, insurance and benefits plans. In 1992, Judy and I moved to Saanichton, BC on Vancouver Island where I opened two businesses, Smith Consulting Group and KittyHawk Securities.

I was fascinated by the fact that Americans were able to deduct the interest on their loans, including their house mortgage loans. One reason that our friends in the USA enjoy a higher life style than we do is because the American home owner has a huge tax deduction to claim each and every year that he owns a mortgage. (An American does start to lose some deductions on anything over a million-dollar mortgage.)

In Canada, house mortgages do not give rise to deductible interest for all but a small percentage of the population. In an attempt to find out more about the rules of tax deductibility, I spent some time with the Tax Act, which is a brutal read.

Who Enjoys Tax Deductible Mortgages in Canada?

The truly wealthy. Plus my clients, most of whom were just ordinary taxpayers like most Canadians. Wealthy people, and all of my clients, are just as likely as you are to have a mortgage on their home. The difference is that the monthly interest portion of their mortgage is tax deductible, and yours is not.

We can learn much from the wealthy. First, they understand leverage. They use OPM – Other People's Money to increase their own wealth. Secondly, any debt they do take on generates big tax deductions because they only borrow to invest. You will recall that the test for deductibility is "what did you do with the money when you borrowed it." Borrow to invest and you can deduct the interest.

It is fashionable in some quarters to denigrate the use of leverage to increase one's wealth, but if you have a house mortgage, you have leveraged. You may have put down as little as 5% to buy a house, borrowing 95% from "Other People" to complete the purchase. And good for you. (Some banks are now offering zero down payment. 100% leveraging!) If you borrow to invest and increase your debt, you are leveraging.

There is a pattern emerging here. Wealthy people intentionally pay for houses, cars, and vacations with their after-tax cash. The not so wealthy, which is 90% of us, borrow the money to buy our houses, cars and vacations.

We do it backwards. At great expense to our future net worth, and our future financial well-being.

Wealthy people borrow money too, but they use it to buy investments such as rental real estate, mutual funds, stocks and bonds. They will also borrow to buy a piece of somebody else's business, or to put into their own business. The rest of the population, which is most of the people in Canada, don't have much money left over at the end of the month with which to invest. When you are paying as much as half of your income in taxes of many kinds, and when you are paying those huge amounts of interest to the bank for your mortgage every month, most Canadians find it very difficult to consider the purchase of investments. So you wait for a better time, such as when the mortgage is retired.

This really hurts your chances of improving your future net worth at a decent rate because the time value of owning investments dictates that the sooner you own them, the more they will compound their value as the years go by. We need a program that allows us to get rid of our non-deductible house mortgage as fast as possible and *simultaneously* we need to be building an investment portfolio as fast as possible. Americans tend to do both things at the same time. Canadians usually wait until the mortgage is gone before they start investing. As you will see, if you use The Smith Manoeuvre, you will be able to do even better than our friends south of the border. You might even move into the wealthy category if you do it right. The Smith Manoeuvre will make this all possible for you.

The wealthy Canadian example, let's call him Eric, may start with a non-deductible loan to buy his house, just like you. But very quickly, his highly paid accountants and lawyers show him one of the tricks of the trade – how to convert the bad-interest mortgage loan to a good-interest investment loan.

Example: Eric may have a new house with a new and non-deductible mortgage for $200,000, just like you. Assume he also has $200,000 worth of mutual funds he has gathered over the years. Eric's tax accountant will be quick to suggest that his client sell his mutual funds, and with the $200,000 cheque he receives, Eric will pay off his brand new mortgage today.

Tomorrow, he will go back to the banker, borrow back $200,000 using the house as collateral, and he will use the borrowed money to buy back $200,000 worth of mutual funds. Eric still has his house, his $200,000 mutual funds and a $200,000 loan, but one important thing is different. Because he borrowed to invest, he has just converted $200,000 of debt from bad debt (non-deductible interest), to good debt (deductible interest). Eric may have some taxes to pay on the sale of the mutual funds, and he may have some commissions to pay for the sale and re-purchase of his mutual funds, but these costs are small potatoes compared to the huge tax deductions he will be getting every year for the rest of his life - free.

At 7%, Eric will have a $14,000 tax deduction this year, next year, and every year that he has the loan, probably to 130 years of age. You won't. Unless you decide to learn how to do The Smith Manoeuvre.

Wealthy people tend not to pay off deductible loans. Why would they? At the 50% tax bracket, the tax department will be sending our wealthy example a cheque for $7,000, tax-free. Every year. You won't get a cheque, <u>even though you both paid the same amount of interest on your loans.</u> The cheque from the tax department is free. It is a gift. There is no tax on it. You can do anything you want with it. It is legal. In fact it is encouraged. You are paying the interest as part of your monthly mortgage payment every month anyway. Why not make it tax deductible? Embrace The Smith Manoeuvre, and your interest will become deductible.

The Rich Get Richer

It doesn't seem too fair, but rather than whimper, let's learn from the wealthy and do our best to emulate their methods. In our example, the debt conversion was done in one day, but there is nothing to prevent persons of more modest means from accomplishing the same results over a longer period of time, by the month.

There are traps to fall into and rules of order to follow so do yourself a favour and retain the services of a financial planner to ensure you optimize your opportunity. For instance, there are rules against selling securities one day then re-purchasing the identical securities within 30 days. If you set your borrowing facilities up in the wrong manner, you could foul up your claim for deductibility as far as the tax department is concerned. It can hurt you to try and do this by yourself. Attempting your own financial planning in these modern times is as dangerous to your health as is taking out your own appendix. Find a real financial planner, one with a designation after his name. These are registered and certified planners who take courses and pass exams. They adhere to a code of ethics.

At our website, www.smithman.net under the tab "Find a Planner" you will find a list of planners who are offering Smith Manoeuvre services in your locale. When you find one you like, get a resume and check with some of the planner's current clients to whom the planner will be pleased to refer you.

This would be a bad juncture in your life to try to do it yourself.

The Objective of The Smith Manoeuvre

The debt of the wealthy generates deductible interest to reduce their tax, which increases their cash flow. They get richer. Your debt, your mortgage, is paid for with your after-tax dollars, and generates no deductible interest. The task at hand is to learn how to do what the wealthy do – convert the mortgage loan from bad debt with non-deductible interest, to good debt where the interest is tax deductible.

Let's Be Clear

To be comfortable with the implementation of The Smith Manoeuvre we need to ensure we understand several very important points:

1.   The Smith Manoeuvre is not a leveraging strategy.

2.   You do not need to increase your debt to get the benefits of The Smith Manoeuvre.

3.   You do not need to spend any of your own cash to get the benefits of The Smith Manoeuvre.

Let's Discuss Leveraging

When you borrow money to invest, your debt rises. Your cash outflow increases to service the increased debt, which is where part of the risk in leveraging comes from.

If you have not increased your debt, you have not leveraged.

Many Canadians will acknowledge that there is risk in borrowing to buy stocks and bonds or mutual funds. They see that leveraging has occurred. Strangely, they feel differently about their mortgage. They are reluctant to acknowledge that leverage has been invoked when they borrowed to buy their home with that 100% bank mortgage. But leveraging has indeed occurred. In fact maximum 100% leveraging has occurred, and debt has increased dramatically by the amount of the mortgage.

Worse, while the interest expense on borrowing for financial investments such as stocks and bonds is tax deductible, the interest on your house mortgage is not.

So, someone with a house mortgage has leveraged their borrowing power into an asset, their home, which means their interest expense is not tax deductible in Canada.

The Smith Manoeuvre is a financial strategy that operates on the assumption that <u>you have already leveraged.</u> If the debt is bad debt, then the best thing you can do is to convert the bad debt to good debt. You will still have debt, but it will change in character from bad debt to good debt. You will begin to receive free tax refund cheques because the interest expense is now tax deductible.

Your debt will not increase during this conversion process, it will remain at the level where it is now.

If the debt does not increase, and it doesn't, no leverage has taken place, and it hasn't.

The Smith Manoeuvre is a debt <u>conversion</u> strategy, not a leveraging strategy.

Levels of Debt

The Smith Manoeuvre makes no recommendation on debt levels for the citizen. The strategy begins with the assumption that you and the bank are satisfied that you can handle the amount of leveraging you have assumed in the mortgage loan you have agreed to service. You have already taken the debt which means you have already leveraged your borrowing power.

Whether you have too much or too little debt is between you and your financial planner. We know with certainty that because it's your house mortgage, the interest expense is not deductible. The Smith Manoeuvre will fix that problem. Without increasing your debt you will learn how to convert your bad loan to a good loan. Simultaneously you will start building a free and clear investment portfolio for your retirement – your personal pension plan. And to make it completely worthwhile, the tax department will begin sending your tax refund cheques that are also tax free.

What Does This Cost Me?

Except for the usual modest expenses associated with setting up financing at your bank, this strategy requires no ongoing cash from your resources. The Smith Manoeuvre is completely self funding. In fact to the contrary, this may be the first financial strategy you have seen where your family actually will begin receiving an annual cash flow that is free and tax free, at the same time. This is new money to your family courtesy of the tax department who will be sending you tax refund cheques, tax free, because your interest expense will start giving you tax deductions to claim.

As somebody once said "I've had bad debt and I've had good debt, and good debt is better."

3

HOW DOES THE SMITH MANOEUVRE WORK?

The Smith Manoeuvre works by converting the bad debt you already have such as your home mortgage, into a good-debt investment loan. Any bad-debt loan can and should be converted into a good-debt loan, but for the purposes of this book we will almost always use an example of an average family, with an average house, an average mortgage and an average income. Conversion of other kinds of non-deductible debt will be covered at the end of this chapter.

Everyone has a different set of financial circumstances to deal with. This book can teach using examples, but it can't produce results specific to the financial circumstances of your own family.

To solve the problem you will be able to utilize my proprietary software The Smithman Calculator referenced in the first chapter. A full range of input variables makes it possible to produce calculations specific to your own personal financial situation at this time of your life. You can play what-if for hours to help you compare various mortgage/investment strategies. There is an order form on the last page of this book for you to photocopy, or you can order on line at *www.smithman.net*.

Let's do a Couple of Examples:

We will input imaginary numbers for two Canadian families using The Smithman Calculator. The first case is the Black family, followed by the Browns. The objective in each case is to have the computer compare the financial difference between utilizing The Smith Manoeuvre and doing things the same old way. You will be surprised by the results.

The Blacks are 40 years of age with both parents working with a total of $100,000 per year joint income. They have a new house and a new mortgage for $200,000. They have two kids so they don't have many other assets yet, but they do manage to put away $500 per month into CSB's, term deposits and GIC's, being conservative folk.

Their program has allowed them to put away a total of $30,000 over the years in CSB's and term deposits as an emergency fund, and they have a $20,000 GIC maturing in 6 months, which is their nest egg. They have some other assets and some RRSPs but these assets are not considered for this exercise. David Chilton wrote a wonderful best seller entitled *The Wealthy Barber* in which the virtues of investing 10% of one's gross income are demonstrated. At $500/mth or $6,000 per year (6% of gross income) going into CSB's, term deposits and GIC's the Blacks are fairly short of David Chilton's target for them of 10% per year, but kids really are expensive, and taxes of all kinds take nearly 50% of everything this family earns.

Most financial planners would be complimentary of this family's efforts thus far.

Summary:

$200,000	mortgage loan amount
40%	marginal tax rate
25 yrs	amortization period
5 yrs	term
7.0%	interest rate of the mortgage
5.0%	interest rate of borrowing to invest
$100,000	total family gross income
10.0%	assumed annual average rate of return on investments
$ 500	monthly purchase of CSB's, term deposits and GIC's
$ 30,000	current value of accumulated CSB's and term deposits
$ 20,000	GIC nest egg, maturing in 6 months.

The Plain Jane Smith Manoeuvre

The Plain Jane Smith Manoeuvre describes the financial strategy of setting up a Smith Manoeuvre at a bank or credit union to do a simple conversion of your debt from bad debt to good debt, in two steps:

Step I

Borrowing back and investing the monthly principal reduction that occurs as you make your monthly mortgage payments over the months remaining on your mortgage. Borrowing the money back creates an investment loan and the interest on this investment loan is tax deductible. You are building an investment portfolio with the borrowed money.

Step II

Each year, when your tax refund arrives, you use this free money to make an extra payment against your mortgage, then you immediately re-borrow and invest the same amount.

That's it. That's all it takes to start the Plain Jane Smith Manoeuvre working for you.

What Difference Does it Make?

Examining the results of Step I using The Smithman Calculator reveals the following:

Results of Step I   *Re-borrow the monthly principal reduction of your mortgage and invest the loan proceeds. (Figure 3.1)*

a. When we run The Smithman Calculator and check-mark the first box for Step I we notice that because of The Smith Manoeuvre, nearly half of the interest expense of $220,241 will turn into tax-deductible interest for the Blacks, a total of $90,400. At the 40% tax bracket, this family will have tax refund cheques totalling $36,160. Free. Not bad for simply rearranging their financing using The Smith Manoeuvre. The tax refund is also tax free.

The SmithMan Calculator

				INSTRUCTIONS
BOOK / WEBSITE	☑ I. Reborrow 1st Mortgage Paydowns, to Invest	☐ IV. Apply Future Recurring Monthly Amounts		
LINKS / FREE	☐ II. Apply Tax Savings To 1st Mortgage, Reborrow to Invest	☐ V. Compare SM to David Chilton's Method		PRINT
FRIEND SEND	☐ III. Apply Liquidated Current Assets	☐ VI. Compare SM to Garth Turner's Method		GRAPH

The Smith Manoeuvre   THE SMITHMAN CALCULATOR   ‹www.smithman.net›

Current Mortgage (Non-deductible Interest)   [RECALCULATE]

Canadian Mortgages - semi annual compounding	▶	
principal	200,000	$
interest rate	7.00	%
amortization in years	25.0	yrs
amortization in months	300	mths
payment	$1,400.83	/ mth

Investment Credit Line (Deductible Interest)

prime rate	4.00	%
prime plus / minus	1.00	%
borrowing rate	5.00	%

Miscellaneous

investment portfolio growth rate	10.00	%
marginal tax rate	40.00	%
annual gross family income	100,000	$
percent of gross income	10.00	%

Recurring Monthly Savings Amounts

eg. Canada Savings Bond	500	$
		$
Total Applied in the Current Calculation		/ mth

Total Income Required to Pay Off Your Current Mortgage

principal in after-tax dollars	$200,000
interest in after-tax dollars	$220,241
total before-tax income your will need to earn	$700,402

Impact of The Smith Manoeuvre on Your Tax Bill

total tax deductions over amortization period	$90,400
total tax deductions via current mortgage	$0
total tax savings using The Smith Manoeuvre	$36,160

Impact of The Smith Manoeuvre on Amortization

current amortization in years	25.00
shortened amortization due to The Smith Manoeuvre	0.00
years saved by The Smith Manoeuvre	0.00

Impact of The Smith Manoeuvre on Your Family Net Worth

value of investment portfolio at end of amortization period	$414,207
offset deductible interest loan	$200,000
net improvement in family net worth	$214,207

Compare The Smith Manoeuvre to David Chilton's Method

future value of Chilton Method PLUS The Smith Manoeuvre	$0
future value of Chilton Method alone	$0
net value of The Smith Manoeuvre over Chilton Method	$0

Compare The Smith Manoeuvre to Garth Turner's Method

future value of The Smith Manoeuvre, net of loan	$0
future value of the Turner Method, net of loan	$0
net value of The Smith Manoeuvre over the Turner Method	$0

Compare The Smith Manoeuvre to Your Current Plan

future value of The Smith Manoeuvre	$214,207
less: future value of (your current plan)	$0
less: future value of V (Chilton's Method)	$0
net value of The Smith Manoeuvre to your family	$214,207

Figure 3.1

b. In addition, assuming for instance that the re-borrowed money was invested in mutual funds earning 10% per year, the pool of funds would stand at $414,207. *These investments are free and clear.* These investments can also be liquid depending on what you decide to buy for your investment portfolio. We use 10% because the 54 year average annual return of the TSE is 10.4%. If you use 8%, the pool would be $305,121. If you use 12% the number is $572,328. (The S+P 500 in the USA averaged 12.5% per year for the past 54 years (Andex) which tells you it may be wise to be diversified by country).

c. To be fair, the original example showed zero debt after 300 months (and zero investments) so we should offset the $200,000 investment loan we are still carrying 25 years later to yield a net improvement of $414,207 - $200,000 = $214,207. This result might attract some taxation if and when you liquidated this investment.

Note on Step I

Notice in Fig 3.1 at the bottom left corner of the screen, there is a box to demonstrate the real cost of a mortgage.

This mortgage will require the owner to pay back $200,000 principal plus 220,241 dollars in interest (non-deductible) for a total of 420,241 dollars. But house mortgages are paid with after-tax dollars, so to understand the true pain of owning a mortgage we need to look at the before-tax cost of the mortgage. This family, at the 40% tax bracket, will have to earn $700,402 to pay off their modest $200,000 mortgage. Nearly three quarters of a million dollars. Do you see why your mortgage is killing you?

Results of Step II   *Apply tax refunds against the first*
                              mortgage, then re-borrow and invest.
                              (Figure 3.2)

a.   The tax savings resulting from the deductible interest
      expense being claimed on your income tax return are
      found money. As found money, generated by The
      Smith Manoeuvre, we have no difficulty getting
      agreement from our clients that these tax savings
      should be applied against the first mortgage, and the
      reduction is immediately re-borrowed and invested.
      Make this agreement with yourself – now.

b.   After Step II is check-marked on the model contained
      in The Smithman Calculator, we see that the tax
      deductions increase to $104,949, thus the tax savings
      refund cheque rises as well, to $41,980, being 40% of the
      deduction.

c.   The mutual fund account grows even more, and
      compounds rapidly, at 10% per year to $509,882. At 8%
      per year it would total $384,896, and at 12%, $688,609.
          We still should offset the fact that we have a $200,000
      tax-deductible loan at the bank, which leaves a net
      improvement in net worth of $309,882. Free.   No
      charge.

d.   As a bonus, the new money available from tax
      refunds, when used to reduce the first mortgage,
      reduces the 25-year amortization period to 22.25 years.

The SmithMan Calculator

BOOK / WEBSITE	☑ I. Reborrow 1st Mortgage Paydowns, to Invest	☐ IV. Apply Future Recurring Monthly Amounts	INSTRUCTIONS
LINKS / FREE	☑ II. Apply Tax Savings To 1st Mortgage. Reborrow to Invest	☐ V. Compare SM to David Chilton's Method	PRINT
FRIEND SEND	☐ III. Apply Liquidated Current Assets	☐ VI. Compare SM to Garth Turner's Method	GRAPH

The Smith Manoeuvre   THE SMITHMAN CALCULATOR   <www.smithman.net>

Current Mortgage (Non-deductible Interest)	**RECALCULATE**		**Impact of The Smith Manoeuvre on Your Tax Bill**	
Canadian Mortgages - semi annual compounding	▶		total tax deductions over amortization period	$104,949
principal	200,000	$	total tax deductions via current mortgage	$0
interest rate	7.00	%	total tax savings using The Smith Manoeuvre	$41,980
amortization in years	25.0	yrs	**Impact of The Smith Manoeuvre on Amortization**	
amortization in months	300	mths	current amortization in years	25.00
payment	$1,400.83	/ mth	shortened amortization due to The Smith Manoeuvre	22.25
Investment Credit Line (Deductible Interest)			years saved by The Smith Manoeuvre	2.75
prime rate	4.00	%	**Impact of The Smith Manoeuvre on Your Family Net Worth**	
prime plus / minus	1.00	%	value of investment portfolio at end of amortization period	$509,882
borrowing rate	5.00	%	offset deductible interest loan	$200,000
Miscellaneous			net improvement in family net worth	$309,882
investment portfolio growth rate	10.00	%	**Compare The Smith Manoeuvre to David Chilton's Method**	
marginal tax rate	40.00	%	future value of Chilton Method PLUS The Smith Manoeuvre	$0
annual gross family income	100,000	$	future value of Chilton Method alone	$0
percent of gross income	10.00	%	net value of The Smith Manoeuvre over Chilton Method	$0
Recurring Monthly Savings Amounts			**Compare The Smith Manoeuvre to Garth Turner's Method**	
eg. Canada Savings Bond	500	$	future value of The Smith Manoeuvre, net of loan	$0
		$	future value of the Turner Method, net of loan	$0
Total Applied in the Current Calculation		/ mth	net value of The Smith Manoeuvre over the Turner Method	$0
Total Income Required to Pay Off Your Current Mortgage			**Compare The Smith Manoeuvre to Your Current Plan**	
principal in after-tax dollars	$220,000		future value of The Smith Manoeuvre	$309,882
interest in after-tax dollars	$220,241		less: future value of (your current plan)	$0
total before-tax income your will need to earn	$700,402		less: future value of V (Chilton's Method)	$0
			net value of The Smith Manoeuvre to your family	$309,882

Figure 3.2

e.   The Smithman Calculator allows you to graph the results of your various inputs. Figure 3.3 is the related graph to Figure 3.2. Notice that the tax deductions paid against the mortgage have reduced the amortization period by 2.75 years.

f.   The tax refunds are received on a tax free basis. Other cheques you receive for work performed or investments sold are likely all taxable. Not this cheque from the CRA.

Note on Step II

These improvements in this family's net worth needed no money from their income. The improvements to the net worth of the Black family, more than $300,000 net, are free to them. This could be your family. Another part of this free increase in wealth is because of free tax deductions that are used to pay down the mortgage, which is then re-borrowed and invested. Part of the increase results from the well understood concept that if you will invest for the long term, your investment gains will be higher than your borrowing costs, especially if your borrowing is for tax deductible purposes.

The salient difference between The Smith Manoeuvre and most other personal investment strategies is that The Smith Manoeuvre brings new money, free, to your family to allow you to speed up the reduction of your non-deductible loans, followed by immediate re-borrowing of the amount paid down. The interest expense of this re-borrowing is tax deductible.

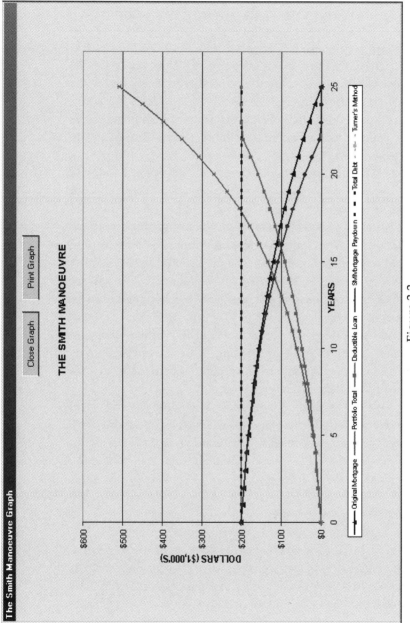

Figure 3.3

The CRA and the Ministry of Finance raised a trial balloon in 2004 regarding the possibility of changing the tax rules regarding interest deductibility. The suggestions generated mountains of responses from professionals across the country with comments ranging from "draconian" to "hare-brained."

If these changes were to be made as proposed, you will be affected as far as your deductions are concerned. But even if the worst happened and it could – government has been doing precious little to help ordinary people -, you will still operate The Smith Manoeuvre. Note the bottom right hand number in Figure 3.1 – the net benefit is $214,207 after checking off Box I. When you go to Figure 3.2, you will see that adding in the effect of tax refunds by checking off Box II raises the return by about $100,000 to $309,882. In other words, two thirds of the effect of The Smith Manoeuvre comes from benefits of owning your investments now instead of later. About one third of the benefit is the effect of converting to tax deductible interest.

We will hate the government if we lose the important benefit of tax deductible interest when we invest and we will vote out the government silly enough to make such an abysmal decision, but we will still continue to operate The Smith Manoeuvre.

That Old Bugbear, Debt

So I have not helped you with your debt. But a different indicator, net worth, is how government, business and wealthy people keep score, not the debt or lack of debt. Debt is but one factor in the measurement of wealth. Proper and judicious utilization of debt is the hallmark of successful governments, vibrant businesses and wealthy individuals. You have debt too, just like the aforementioned groups. The difference is, theirs is tax deductible and yours is not. The effect is hugely negative for you, hugely positive for them. Too much debt, deductible or otherwise is a big mistake.

Have You Heard of Tax Freedom Day?

Go to www.fraserinstitute.ca to read about Tax Freedom Day. This is simply the day of the year that you stopped working for the three levels of government and started working for you. It is made up of all the different taxes we pay to support government. Some of our taxes go to important things we need such as roads, health and defence. Huge amounts are also required to fund the waste and corruption such as the Adscam affair.

In 2004, Tax Freedom Day occurred on June 28th – nearly half the year you worked for governments. So nearly 50% of your annual gross income goes to taxes of all kinds. 25 to 30% goes to shelter. If you only have 20 or 25% of your income left to pay for food, clothing, education, recreation, savings, retirement, transportation, etc., etc., is it any wonder that the money runs out before the month runs out? Is it any wonder that about one third of Canadians cannot afford to buy an RRSP? It's tough out there. One of the best ways to improve your future is to reduce your taxes. One of the best ways to reduce your taxes is to ensure you make your interest expense tax deductible. Just like wealthy people do.

Like the government, companies and wealthy folk are not immune to forgetting the rules when it comes to the use of debt – too much debt can bite.

The point is this – you already have the debt in the form of your house mortgage. My thesis is simply that you can pick up large improvements in net worth for your family by *converting* the debt you already have. *The Smith Manoeuvre does not require you to increase your debt.*

Even if your debt is reasonable in the amount of it, if it's standard home mortgage debt, it's the wrong kind of debt. The negative effect of debt is offset in magnificent fashion when you convert it from bad debt to good debt. Do this first. Get your debt converted using The Smith Manoeuvre, and once that's done, decide whether you want to hold it level for the next 100 years of your life, or reduce it. It is your choice. It won't take much time to complete the conversion, especially if you take the additional actions recommended further along in this book.

Steps I and II are the essence of what is unique and original about The Smith Manoeuvre. Step III is a strategy routinely employed by the wealthy. This is called Debt Swapping and is not a new concept. A B.C. accountant has been very public over the last quarter century popularizing the concept of debt swapping on radio and in print. He is David Ingram, and you can hear him on Sunday morning radio on Fred Snyder's popular financial affairs program on AM radio 600 at 9:00 am. Combining these steps will increase your wealth.

The Enhanced Plain Jane Smith Manoeuvre

Steps I and II make up The Plain Jane Smith Manoeuvre. We can develop even larger net worth by adding two more steps. These two new steps, like the first two still do not require you to contribute any new money, nor does any new money need to be borrowed. All four steps together produce the Enhanced Plain Jane Smith Manoeuvre.

Step III (The Debt Swap Accelerator)

Reduce your 1st mortgage using cash obtained by liquidating any available term deposits, CSB's, GIC's, mutual funds, stocks and bonds or other paid up assets you own, *and then* borrow back the same amount to invest in replacement assets.

Step IV (The Cash Flow Diversion Accelerator)

Divert current monthly savings and investment plan amounts against the first mortgage, *and then* borrow back the same amount to invest.

Let's quantify the nice words with nice numbers using The Smithman Calculator. By checking off the box at Step III, the numbers look rather dramatic. The excellent results stem from the benefits of liquidating the $30,000 and $20,000 assets and using the proceeds to reduce the first mortgage so the Blacks can re-borrow to invest.

Results of Step III   *Lump sum reductions of first mortgage. (Figure 3.4)*

The tax deductions have now jumped from $104,949 to $195,552. At the 40% tax bracket, the tax savings have also jumped from $41,980 to $78,221 – nearly double.

The SmithMan Calculator

BOOK / WEBSITE   ☑ I. Reborrow 1st Mortgage Paydowns, to Invest   ☐ IV. Apply Future Recurring Monthly Amounts   **INSTRUCTIONS**

LINKS / FREE   ☑ II. Apply Tax Savings To 1st Mortgage. Reborrow to Invest   ☐ V. Compare SM to David Chilton's Method   **PRINT**

FRIEND SEND   ☑ III. Apply Liquidated Current Assets $50,000   ☐ VI. Compare SM to Garth Turner's Method   **GRAPH**

The Smith Manoeuvre	THE SMITHMAN CALCULATOR	<www.smithman.net>

Current Mortgage (Non-deductible Interest)   **RECALCULATE** ▶

Canadian Mortgages - semi annual compounding ▶		
principal	200,000	$
interest rate	7.00	%
amortization in years	25.0	yrs
amortization in months	300	mths
payment	$1,400.83	/ mth

Investment Credit Line (Deductible Interest)

prime rate	4.00	%
prime plus / minus	1.00	%
borrowing rate	5.00	%

Miscellaneous

investment portfolio growth rate	10.00	%
marginal tax rate	40.00	%
annual gross family income	100,000	$
percent of gross income	10.00	%

Recurring Monthly Savings Amounts

eg. Canada Savings Bond	500	$
		$
Total Applied in the Current Calculation		/ mth

Total Income Required to Pay Off Your Current Mortgage

principal in after-tax dollars	$200,000
interest in after-tax dollars	$220,241
total before-tax income your will need to earn	$700,402

Impact of The Smith Manoeuvre on Your Tax Bill

total tax deductions over amortization period	$195,552
total tax deductions via current mortgage	$0
total tax savings using The Smith Manoeuvre	$78,221

Impact of The Smith Manoeuvre on Amortization

current amortization in years	25.00
shortened amortization due to The Smith Manoeuvre	12.08
years saved by The Smith Manoeuvre	12.92

Impact of The Smith Manoeuvre on Your Family Net Worth

value of investment portfolio at end of amortization period	$1,409,709
offset deductible interest loan	$200,000
net improvement in family net worth	$1,209,709

Compare The Smith Manoeuvre to David Chilton's Method

future value of Chilton Method PLUS The Smith Manoeuvre	$0
future value of Chilton Method alone	$0
net value of The Smith Manoeuvre over Chilton Method	$0

Compare The Smith Manoeuvre to Garth Turner's Method

future value of The Smith Manoeuvre, net of loan	$0
future value of the Turner Method, net of loan	$0
net value of The Smith Manoeuvre over the Turner Method	$0

Compare The Smith Manoeuvre to Your Current Plan

future value of The Smith Manoeuvre	$1,209,709
less: future value of III sums (your current plan)	$541,735
less: future value of V (Chilton's Method)	$0
net value of The Smith Manoeuvre to your family	$667,974

Figure 3.4

In addition, instead of taking 25 years to get rid of the mortgage, it is now paid off in less than half the time at 12.08 years. Best of all, the investment fund, purchased with borrowed funds so that the interest expense will be deductible, is much larger at $1,409,709 at 10% annual rate of return. (You still need to offset $200,000 in recognition that we still have that deductible interest loan on the books.) At 8%, the value of the fund is $971,691, and at 12% it is $2,081,345. To input lump sums at different months into the future, you will use a pop-up panel that appears when you click on Check Box III in The Smithman Calculator software.

Note on Step III

After tax and after inflation, the CSB's and term deposits of $30,000 and the $20,000 GIC, are terrible investments. They earn a pittance in interest and attract full tax on the earnings, which has to be paid every year. Big tax on small interest is not good for your financial well being.

Many financial planners are still doling out the advice that you should have the equivalent of three to six months' income in a CSB or term deposit in case of an emergency. I've been at this business for over 20 years and I've met precious few families who have had such an emergency, number one. Number two, in case you do have an emergency, be covered by a "no-touchy" creditline to handle any such eventuality. It costs nothing unless you use it.

Number three, you should sell your CSB's and term deposits, apply the proceeds against your first mortgage, and borrow back the identical amount to purchase a real investment. If you invest in stocks, bonds, mutual funds, investment real estate, somebody else's business or your own business, the interest expense will be tax deductible. You are borrowing with the expectation of earning income from your investments.

You could do the conversion of the debt all in one day if you had enough assets. (The Blacks have $30,000 to deal with now and $20,000 in six months.) By suppertime the Blacks will still be protected by their new creditline for that potential emergency, their mortgage will have been knocked down by $30,000, they will have bought back $30,000 in investments and because they borrowed to invest, the interest is tax deductible. Same for the $20,000 nest egg, six months from now.

So their debt stayed the same (bad debt down, good debt up by exactly the same amount), their less-than-mediocre assets in the form of CSB's, term deposits and GIC's have been replaced by some form of equities or perhaps investment real estate.

In addition the Blacks are generating free tax refund cheques because their mortgage interest, which they were paying anyway, has now been turned into tax deductible interest because the interest is being charged on an investment loan, not a housing loan.

Results of Step IV   *Diverting   monthly   savings   and investment amounts. (Figure 3.5)*

When we check-mark box IV on The Smithman Calculator, we find all results in each category have increased again. Tax deductions have increased to $215,011

The SmithMan Calculator

BOOK / WEBSITE	☑ I. Reborrow 1st Mortgage Paydowns, to Invest	☑ IV. Apply Future Recurring Monthly Amounts	INSTRUCTIONS
LINKS / FREE	☑ II. Apply Tax Savings To 1st Mortgage, Reborrow to Invest	☐ V. Compare SM to David Chilton's Method	PRINT
FRIEND SEND	☑ III. Apply Liquidated Current Assets $50,000	☐ VI. Compare SM to Garth Turner's Method	GRAPH

The Smith Manoeuvre   　　THE SMITHMAN CALCULATOR　　　<www.smithman.net>

Current Mortgage (Non-deductible Interest)

RECALCULATE ▶		
Canadian Mortgages - semi annual compounding		
principal	200,000	$
interest rate	7.00	%
amortization in years	25.0	yrs
amortization in months	300	mths
payment	$1,400.83	/ mth

Investment Credit Line (Deductible Interest)

prime rate	4.00	%
prime plus / minus	1.00	%
borrowing rate	5.00	%

Miscellaneous

investment portfolio growth rate	10.00	%
marginal tax rate	40.00	%
annual gross family income	100,000	$
percent of gross income	10.00	%

Recurring Monthly Savings Amounts

eg. Canada Savings Bond	500	$
		$
Total Applied in the Current Calculation	$500	/ mth

Total Income Required to Pay Off Your Current Mortgage

principal in after-tax dollars	$200,000
interest in after-tax dollars	$220,241
total before-tax income your will need to earn	$700,402

Impact of The Smith Manoeuvre on Your Tax Bill

total tax deductions over amortization period	$215,011
total tax deductions via current mortgage	$0
total tax savings using The Smith Manoeuvre	$86,004

Impact of The Smith Manoeuvre on Amortization

current amortization in years	25.00
shortened amortization due to The Smith Manoeuvre	8.08
years saved by The Smith Manoeuvre	16.92

Impact of The Smith Manoeuvre on Your Family Net Worth

value of investment portfolio at end of amortization period	$2,162,770
offset deductible interest loan	$200,000
net improvement in family net worth	$1,962,770

Compare The Smith Manoeuvre to David Chilton's Method

future value of Chilton Method PLUS The Smith Manoeuvre	$0
future value of Chilton Method alone	$0
net value of The Smith Manoeuvre over Chilton Method	$0

Compare The Smith Manoeuvre to Garth Turner's Method

future value of The Smith Manoeuvre, net of loan	$0
future value of the Turner Method, net of loan	$0
net value of The Smith Manoeuvre over the Turner Method	$0

Compare The Smith Manoeuvre to Your Current Plan

future value of The Smith Manoeuvre	$1,962,770
less: future value of III + IV sums (your current plan)	$1,205,152
less: future value of V (Chilton's Method)	$0
net value of The Smith Manoeuvre to your family	$757,618

Figure 3.5

and the tax refunds will now be $86,004 instead of $78,221 after Step III.

We will be out of this mortgage in 8.08 years instead of 25 years. Most amazingly, the mutual fund jumps to $2,162,770 (less the $200,000 loan we are still carrying because it is a tax deductible loan) for a total net worth improvement of $1,962,770 after 300 months. It may sound improbable, but you will find that the arithmetic is accurate. At 8% the pool is $1,509,878, and at 12% it is $3,149,252.

Note on Step IV

Over the years the Blacks have been saving 6% of their gross income to build up an emergency fund, as well as a nest egg for the future. They have not had much in the way of financial training, so the $500 per month is put into CSB's and term deposits in their emergency fund account and a portion of the cash is used to buy a GIC for their nest egg.

They should divert these monthly amounts in order to reduce their first mortgage. As soon as this is done, they will borrow the same amount of money back from the bank, and get it invested. I will share my opinions on what kind of investments in the next chapter.

Comparing the Smith Manoeuvre Way to The Usual Way

The Blacks took four easy steps, reorganized their financial set up, converted their bad debt to the good kind, and now they are sitting on assets of nearly two million dollars.

Albert Einstein was asked what he would consider the eighth Wonder of the World, and apparently he said "compound interest". These numbers could be your numbers. It's easy to do. It's important to do. We indicated that this was a comparison between two methods. Accordingly, we need to calculate where the Blacks would end up financially if they *did not* engage The Smith Manoeuvre. It's the difference that counts, because the results of both methods are exciting. One is more exciting than the other.

Figure 3.6 summarizes and compares results for the difference in net worth for the Blacks doing it their way, and doing it The Smith Manoeuvre way.

What About Lower Income Families?

Here is a Smith Manoeuvre comparison for a younger family just getting in gear, the Browns.

$100,000	mortgage loan amount
30%	marginal tax rate
25 yrs	amortization period
5 yrs	term
7.0%	interest rate of the mortgage
5.0%	interest rate of borrowing to invest
$ 50,000	total family gross income
10.0%	assumed annual average rate of return on investments
$ 200	monthly purchase of CSB's
$ 5,000	current value of accumulated CSB's.

COMPARATIVE STRATEGY SUMMARIES FOR THE BLACK FAMILY

Fig 3.6

A. The usual way - pay off the mortgage to zero, while investing as much cash as possible for 25 years, at 10%.

	Debt		Tax			Net Worth After 25 Yrs.		
	Start	End	Deductions	Refunds	Time	Investments	Debt	Net Worth
Current mortgage	200,000	0	0	0	25 yrs	-	-	-
Current savings - $50,000	-	-	0	0	25 yrs	541,735	0	541,735
Monthly savings - $500	-	-	0	0	25 yrs	663,417	0	663,417
								$1,205,152

B. The Smith Manoeuvre way - convert the bad debt to good debt, re-borrow to invest, generate tax deductions to apply against the mortgage to increase deductible borrowing for investments, for 25 years at 10%.

	Debt		Tax			Net Worth After 25 Yrs.		
	Start	End	Deductions	Refunds	Time	Investments	Debt	Net Worth
After Step I	200,000	200,000	90,400	36,120	25.00 yrs	414,207	200,000	214,207
After Step II	200,000	200,000	104,949	41,980	22.25 yrs	509,882	200,000	309,882
After Step III	200,000	200,000	195,552	78,221	12.08 yrs	1,409,709	200,000	1,209,709
After Step IV	200,000	200,000	215,011	86,005	8.08 yrs	2,162,770	200,000	1,962,770
								$1,962,770

C. Summary

Assuming the same starting position for each strategy regarding debt, time, investment rate of return, monthly investment amounts and current investment values, The Smith Manoeuvre has increased the future value of the Black's net worth from $1,205,152 to $1,962,770. This is a difference of $757,618, which represents an improvement of 62%.

The methodologies are exactly the same as the prior case. The results are even more striking for this lower income family. On a proportionate basis, the Browns do better than the Blacks. The results of The Plain Jane Smith Manoeuvre (Step I and Step II) are free for the asking, courtesy of the taxman plus compounding assets. The Enhanced Plain Jane Smith Manoeuvre (adding Steps III and IV) will improve the family's future net worth even more, simply by employing existing paid-up current assets and future planned savings in a more important way.

Note: In the Enhanced Plain Jane Smith Manoeuvre for both the Blacks and the Browns, the investment vehicles they owned that could be liquidated were Canada Savings Bonds, term deposits or Guaranteed Investment Certificates. Upon liquidation, so that proceeds could be utilized to pay down their existing first mortgage, the full value was available for mortgage reduction. This is because these instruments have already paid income tax on their gains every year. It should be noted that if they were liquidating mutual funds, real estate or stock, there might be some income tax to pay in the year of sale, reducing by some amount the funds available for mortgage reduction. This is another reason you should locate a financial planner to assist with the set-up of The Smith Manoeuvre.

Figure 3.7 summarizes and compares results for the difference in net worth for the Browns doing it their way, and doing it The Smith Manoeuvre way.

This large improvement in this family's net worth is a consequence of free tax deductions generated by The Smith Manoeuvre, which are subsequently used to speed up the conversion period from bad debt to good debt. There is a

Fig 3.7

COMPARATIVE STRATEGY SUMMARIES FOR THE BROWN FAMILY

A. The usual way - pay off the mortgage to zero, while investing as much cash as possible for 25 years at 10%.

	Debt		Tax			Net Worth After 25 Yrs.		
	Start	End	Deductions	Refunds	Time	Investments	Debt	Net Worth
Current mortgage	100,000	0	0	0	25 yrs	-	-	-
Current savings - $5,000	-	-	0	0	25 yrs	54,174	0	54,174
Monthly savings - $200	-	-	0	0	25 yrs	265,367	0	265,367
								$319,541

B. The Smith Manoeuvre way - convert the bad debt to good debt, re-borrow to invest, generate tax deductions to apply against the mortgage to increase deductible borrowing for investment, for 25 years at 10%.

	Debt		Tax			Net Worth After 25 Yrs.		
	Start	End	Deductions	Refunds	Time	Investments	Debt	Net Worth
After Step I	100,000	100,000	45,200	13,560	25.00 yrs	207,103	100,000	107,103
After Step II	100,000	100,000	50,849	15,255	22.83 yrs	242,086	100,000	142,086
After Step III	100,000	100,000	65,129	19,539	19.92 yrs	335,962	100,000	235,962
After Step IV	100,000	100,000	89,485	26,845	12.67 yrs	666,541	100,000	566,541
								$566,541

C. Summary

Assuming the same starting position for each strategy regarding debt, time, investment rate of return, monthly investment amounts and current investment values, The Smith Manoeuvre has increased the future value of the Brown's net worth from $319,541 to $566,541. This is a difference of $247,000, which represents an improvement of 77%.

significant second advantage that automatically derives when you use The Smith Manoeuvre to shorten the amortization period of your bad-debt mortgage. Your mortgage "payment efficiency" is increased.

Payment efficiency refers to the jump in the amount of principal reduction that occurs in the next and subsequent payments following a payment of principal against a mortgage. The amount of the payments being compared is the same, but if a lump sum reduction occurs between payments, the ratio of principal reduction to interest paid is noticeably improved in the next payment and all future payments. The mortgage amortization period is thus shortened. In Figure 3.8, we can see the payment efficiency phenomenon in action.

A	B	C	D	E	F	G
			Monthly Payment			
End of Mth	Loan Balance $200,000	Lump Sum Pmt	Principal Reduction	Int Exp	Total Pmt (D+E)	Efficiency Ratio (D÷F)
1	199,749	0	251	1,150	1,401	17.92%
2	169,497	30,000	252	1,149	1,401	17.99
3	169,071	0	426	975	1,401	30.41
4	168,642	0	429	972	1,401	30.62

Figure 3.8

This table shows the first four months of a $200,000 mortgage for 25 years at 7%. The payment for 25 years is $1,400.83 per month. Notice that the first payment reduces the principal by only $251. The interest cost (non-deductible) is $1,150. In month two, the principal reduction is a dollar more at $252 because the total loan was $251 less this month than last month. It dropped from $199,749 to $199,497.

The homeowner then read about The Smith Manoeuvre, and realized that their $30,000 savings account should be liquidated to make a lump sum reduction of the mortgage. In month three, the same payment of $1,401 reduced the principal by $426 which is $174 more than the previous month. The efficiency of the regular mortgage payment increased from 17.99% ($252/$1,401) to 30.41% ($426/$1,401).

Any extra money applied against your mortgage over and above your regular payment increases the payment efficiency of all future mortgage payments. The result is that you will pay your mortgage off sooner.

Shorter is better when paying off mortgages, right?

What About Other Non-Deductible Loans?

Any loan on which the interest expense is not deductible can and should be converted to deductible interest.

If you have non-deductible consumer loans they very likely charge interest at a rate some points above the prime rate. Credit card and department store debt cost many points above prime. If you set up The Smith Manoeuvre 75% investment creditline, and if you have more than 25% equity in your home, you may be well advised to use some of your new credit to consolidate your non-deductible loans. The process entails having two creditlines instead of one. One will represent your non-deductible interest consolidation loan and the other will be the 75% deductible-interest investment creditline. The bank will lend you 75% of the value of your house, for investment purposes, less the total owed on your first mortgage and less the amount of the consolidation loan.

If your first mortgage alone is at 75%, you can start The Smith Manoeuvre, but you will not have room for consolidation of any other debt. You can and should still take steps to convert the debt of your non-deductible loans. It may be possible to combine these loans into a simple loan as an initial step, without involving the equity in your home which we are assuming sits at 25% in this example. Let's say you have a $20,000 car loan and a $10,000 credit card balance. Perhaps you can arrange to combine the loans into one $30,000 non-deductible interest loan as Step 1.

For Step 2, you will want to set up The Mini Smith Manoeuvre.

Executing The Mini Smith Manoeuvre

Step 1

Speak with the loans manager of the bank that holds your loans.

Step 2

Explain that your objective is to convert your non-deductible interest car loan to a deductible-interest creditline for investment purposes. If your car loan is for $30,000, your plan is to open an investment creditline of $30,000. If your credit is good enough, you will be granted the creditline on an unsecured basis.

Step 3

If the banker requests security, offer the car. But the car is already security for the original outstanding car loan. That's ok, because you can agree that the two loan totals added together will not rise above $30,000. For example, you agree that if you want to borrow $5,000 to invest, you will not be able to do so until you have reduced the car loan by $5,000. In this arrangement the banker feels safe, and justified in using the car as security for both loans, because added together, the total indebtedness is only $30,000 or less, never more.

Step 4

If the banker is still leery, offer the security of the car loan *plus* the investments you intend to purchase. This should do it – he is now double secured.

Step 5

If your banker has not cooperated by now, advise him you are going shopping. A few phone calls will provide you names of bankers who are happy to provide this mini version of The Smith Manoeuvre. Remember, it's no skin off a banker's nose to give you this service.

1. You are not increasing your debt; you are converting if from the bad kind to the good kind.

2. You are offering the bank the same or better security.

3. You will have additional assets/wealth that neither you nor the banker contemplated before you read this book. If you are better off, the bank's loan with you is safer. He likes that.

4. The cash benefits you begin receiving now are not paid by the banker, they are paid by the taxman. *This is an extra, tax-free income* for your family.

5. Your car loan is your liability, but it is the bank's asset. Every day, as millions of Canadians make their car payments, the assets of the banks are declining. You are offering your banker a solution – give you The Mini Smith Manoeuvre, and for at least a few years, your loan, his asset, will stay level while you engineer the conversion of your debt from the bad kind to the good kind. And if you like the way The Mini Smith Manoeuvre is improving your financial well being, he might just end up happily still holding your loan when finally you exit this world at age 130. Why would you ever pay off this beautiful tax-deductible interest loan? But that's your decision to make, at a later date, certainly no sooner than the time it takes to make all that interest into on-going tax deductions.

The Mini Smith Manoeuvre is what you use to convert those miscellaneous non-deductible loans into juicy tax deductions.

So take some time to map out your work plan, then get at it so you can bring these financial savings home for your family to enjoy.

4

WEALTH ACCUMULATION

Saving vs. Investing

In the Black's case, the accumulation of savings has occurred because prior to now they have been diverting 6% of their gross income each month to buy CSB's, term deposits and GIC's. These are savings systems as opposed to investment systems. The Blacks are lending their hard earned after-tax dollars to government or big businesses, such as the banks. In return they earn a very low rate of interest, and then at the end of the year, whatever small amount they did earn is taxed at 40%. So a bad investment is made worse.

On the other hand, these savings vehicles are safe. Even if the government is broke, they can always raise your taxes to get enough money from you, to give you back the small percentage they need to give you as your interest, then at the end of the year they will tax you at 40% on what they gave you for interest, which they got from you in taxes. The final humiliation is that your miniscule return on investment must then be depreciated by the inflation rate. This assumes you are interested in knowing the real rate of return. When you see it is negative, as in the case of Canada Savings Bonds, maybe your interest will turn to annoyance. So you are "safe"... safely losing money, that is.

News item, Financial Post, Tuesday, October 5th, 2004 by Jonathan Chevreau. NEW CSB'S PAY LESS THAN INFLATION. "The new series of Canada Savings Bonds went on sale yesterday, boasting a miniscule 1.35% interest rate, which doesn't even match the inflation rate."

So your federal government is taking money off of you knowing you desire safety, and the rate you receive is less than inflation.

But it's worse than that. The paltry interest they pay you is taxable every year. If you are at the 40% tax bracket, that means that after tax you will only have 0.81% - less than 1% (1.35 x 0.40 = 0.54 = tax. 1.35 − 0.54 = 0.81 = after-tax return before inflation). With inflation at around 2%, then after tax and after inflation you are losing more than 1% on your Canada Savings Bonds. But you are losing your money safely.

The article ends with this comment: "while not competitive with inflation, the new crop of CSB's are in line with current GIC's offered by the banks." Now you feel a lot better.

To Learn More

There is a wonderful company called Andex in Windsor, Ontario that makes all kinds of charts comparing the performances of the stock markets against the money markets, including 5 year GIC's, long term bonds, and 90 day Canada T-Bills (visit them at _www.andexcharts.com_).

If these debt style instruments are losing money, what should you invest in?

Investing in Real Estate

You could buy investment real estate, which might be better than investing in debt instruments. Might be. Many excellent business writers point to three pressures on real estate as an investment class:

1. It is not a very liquid investment.

2. Prices for houses across much of Canada are generally too high such that it is difficult to consistently earn decent profit margins when operating them as rentals. This is because rents traditionally do not rise in direct proportion to the increase in the capital cost of the property. A $100,000 revenue house in 1980 might have brought in $800 per month. Now that the rental has doubled in value to $200,000, it hurts that the rental house only commands $1,200 in rent. The capital tied up has doubled, but the rent income has only grown by 50%.

3. It is broadly forecast by demographers and financial experts such as Garth Turner that as the baby boomers start to retire, some will downsize. It does not take too much of a surplus in any one price band to reduce prices across the board. In addition, the number of homebuyers coming on stream is a much smaller cohort than the cohort that is getting ready to retire. This translates to less than normal demand. This double negative does not bode well for single-family residential investment housing

once the baby boomers start to retire "en bloc" in a few years time.

4. Investment housing over the long term has usually managed to match or exceed inflation by a modest margin. Your own home generally does better than revenue houses because your home is free of capital gains tax and revenue properties are not. If you already own your home, perhaps the siren call of diversification will convince you that it's time to add financial investments to your portfolio instead of more real estate.

If money market debt investments are negative and if rental properties are marginal, what is there left to invest in?

Despite the shock of the dot com bust and the mess of crooked companies getting caught in their tawdry escapades, it looks as though investment in equities is still the best bet for the bulk of your investing, based on historic rates of return on investment.

It's not much fun sometimes, but if we know that doing nothing is a losing proposition, and if we know debt instruments are not much better than breakeven, and if we do comprehend the realities that will likely come to real estate because of the laws of supply and demand, then perhaps it's equities by default.

Equities have always done well if you stay invested and ignore the volatility. If you have no plans to sell your house, then it tends to matter little to you if house prices are dropping or rising – you don't pay much attention. We should learn to do the same with equity investments.

It is interesting to use the Andex Charts to make comparisons of equities similar to the comparisons I made for debt instruments.

Over the same 54 years, the TSE has averaged an annual return of 10.4%. In the best light, assuming the earnings for all those years were reinvested capital gains, then today's figure would be 10.4% for both before-tax and after-tax considerations because you would pay no tax until the securities were sold. You would still subtract inflation of 4.1% to yield 6.3%, which is rather excellent.

While it is possible to own 100% tax efficient equities as in the prior example, in reality, most portfolios will have some taxation occurring each year. There is no doubt that you would bet on equities over debt investments on most any day of the year while in your working years. As we get older we may feel we have to take less return in order to increase the safety of our capital.

Some will say that equities are too volatile. The scenario we paint for users of The Smith Manoeuvre is that when they invest in equities, they should be broadly diversified in different asset classes, they should lean to blue chip and they should invest early, regularly and often. If they follow this advice they avoid trying to time the market. At least until they have the ability to predict the future.

Volatility does not hurt us if we are not trying to time the market. The Andex Charts show that in no decade beginning with 1950 has the ten-year average dropped below 10% per year for the TSE.

The equivalent 54-year performance for the Standard and Poor index in the USA is 12.5%, which is 20.2% better than Canada's stock market performance. This is evidence to further support the common sense notion that we should be investing in several countries of the world if we want to increase returns and decrease risk.

What's Important Here?

Regardless of whether you agree about what kind of investing is best for you, it should be noted that your net worth will improve in large amounts when you liquidate current assets, use the proceeds to over-pay your mortgage, then borrow back to repurchase the assets you sold, or better ones. (Be aware that you can't sell and repurchase the *identical* asset within 30 days of the sale.) Ask your financial planner or accountant to explain the superficial loss rules to you.

What About RRSPs?

Most but not all financial advisors agree that an RRSP is a useful and profitable device for most Canadians. There has been a long and continuous battle raging on the question "Is it better to use after tax dollars to buy an RRSP or to make an extra payment on the mortgage?"

It's good that the amount you contribute is tax deductible. It's bad that you must use after-tax dollars to buy the RRSP. It's good that the investments inside the RRSP can grow tax free. It's bad that RRSP investments are taxed as 100% income when you de-register them. On and on it goes.

The nay sayers point to the fact that more than one third of eligible Canadians don't have an RRSP, and that most RRSP's are meagre in size. My personal opinion is that the reason so many have no RRSP or have small RRSP's has more to do with affordability than an aversion to RRSP's. Many people cannot afford them. So, there is much discussion on whether or not to RRSP. This animated discourse has been going on for years. Google "RRSP or mortgage" and you will find hundreds of articles arguing both sides of the issue. (Many give up and solve the puzzle by suggesting you buy an RRSP instead of paying down your mortgage, then they suggest you apply your RRSP tax refund against your mortgage.)

These hundreds of articles have been written without prior consideration of the natural positive effects we have seen that emanate from utilizing The Smith Manoeuvre. In many, but not all cases, it appears that a Canadian should choose to set up The Smith Manoeuvre, cash the RRSP, pay the tax, use the residue to make a lump sum reduction of the first mortgage then immediately borrow back that money and invest it outside the RRSP. If this is a profitable step, then it also says that current monthly cash flow that is buying RRSP's should cease. Instead it should be applied as over payments against the mortgage.

The mortgage would obviously be converted to deductible much quicker in this scenario. As soon as the conversion was accomplished so that all debt was now deductible, monthly RRSP purchases would resume.

There are so many variables involved when dealing with RRSP's and mortgages simultaneously that it is impossible to make blanket recommendations. Accordingly I suggest that first you get your Smith Manoeuvre up and running. Then you and your financial planner can take the time to analyze your specific circumstances to determine whether you are financially better off to sell or hold your RRSP during your mortgage conversion period.

The comparison of before-tax and after-tax incomes is an important way to analyze correctly the impact of financial decisions we need to make in life. A very important booklet on this subject *Dispelling the Myths of Borrowing to Invest* has been written by one of Canada's up and coming financial gurus, Talbot Stevens. Read about him, and order his book via his website at *www.talbotstevens.com*.

Summary

The Smith Manoeuvre does not require that you choose one asset class over another. The strategy provides investment cash flow starting immediately. You will choose which assets you want to gather at which time and in which order. We encourage diversification, but that is your decision to make. We encourage blue-chip, but maybe your pleasure quotient arising from risk taking is more important to you than surety of capital.

Your eligibility to organize The Smith Manoeuvre has already occurred. The bank has already determined you are a decent credit risk – they gave you a mortgage. Assuming your credit is still satisfactory, you will ensure that the banker understands you are not requesting increased credit – you simply desire to <u>convert</u> the bad debt you currently have with him, to the good debt you deserve.

You may be starting to feel comfortable that The Smith Manoeuvre seems logical and reasonable in its claims. This would be the time to suggest you corroborate your intuition by comparing mathematical comparisons of Your Way versus The Smith Manoeuvre Way. To see how much your future will be improved, all you need do is input your personal assumptions and mortgage facts into The

Smithman Calculator. The improvement in wealth accumulation that is engineered by The Smith Manoeuvre will surprise you. These excellent improvements required no new cash flow from you. Your gains do not require you to increase your debt either. Debt levels do not have to get any higher than where they are when you start the program. The Smith Manoeuvre is totally self funding. Even the cost of the interest expense (deductible) on your new investment creditline is allowed for. The software is very powerful and is designed to calculate and reserve the amount of interest needed to service the investment line. This expense is accommodated out of the amount of principal reduction that occurs when a mortgage payment is paid. The difference is the actual amount that is available to be invested each month.

What If You Move?

A concern for some readers might revolve around the intent to change homes in the future. Do not let that prospect dissuade you from implementing The Smith Manoeuvre now, even if you know you may be moving. The strategy is completely portable at the bank where a routine process called Substitution of Collateral will be utilized to ensure your deductible loans stay deductible. Your planner and your banker will work together to keep you enjoying the benefits of The Smith Manoeuvre.

With the value of doing The Smith Manoeuvre quantified, it is time to round out our understanding of interest expense in Canada.

5

INTEREST EXPENSE

Deductible versus Non-Deductible Interest

In some countries such as the United States, most loan interest paid by a taxpayer may be deducted from other income at tax-filing time regardless of what purpose the money was borrowed for in the first place. This generates a tax refund cheque to the favour of the American taxpayer.

In Canada, the tax department is not so generous. Interest paid on money borrowed to buy the family car, vacations, cottages, credit card consolidation and "general consumption" cannot be deducted from other income for purposes of calculating income tax. No tax refund cheque for the Canadian taxpayer.

More importantly, interest on the largest loan many Canadians will ever take out, their house mortgage, is also not tax deductible. This is a huge disadvantage to Canadians.

How Huge?

If a Canadian family and an American family have both taken out a $200,000 mortgage with a 25 year amortization and 7% interest, each family will have to repay the $200,000 principal amount borrowed, plus approximately an additional $220,000 in interest expense. This totals about $420,000.

The American may deduct the $220,000 interest expense from his other income, and at a 40% tax rate, the American will receive an $88,000 tax refund over the life of the mortgage. Assume he invests his tax refunds and earns 10% per year for 25 years, and you will begin to understand how important it is to make interest tax deductible whenever you can. That's because the invested tax refunds will generate about $700,000 for our American friend.

The Canadian has to pay back the full $420,000 too, but with no tax refunds, and therefore no investments are possible. Worse than that, the full $420,000 for our disadvantaged Canadian will be paid with after-tax dollars. At the 40% tax bracket that means our hapless citizen will have to earn $700,000, pay income tax at 40%, which is $280,000, in order to be able to have $420,000 with which to pay the principal and interest on his tiny $200,000 mortgage loan. It must be coming clear to the reader that it is critical to find a way to convert your mortgage interest into a tax deduction if you live in Canada. Want to know what your equivalent numbers are? They are calculated for you automatically as a function of the software contained in The Smithman Calculator.

To be fair, it should be pointed out that in Canada, we enjoy tax-free capital gains if we make a profit when we sell our home. In the States, a portion of the capital gains that might occur upon sale of the principal residence is taxed. This is a modest offset - if you could choose between deductible interest or tax free capital gains, you would take deductible interest.

If you employ The Smith Manoeuvre, you will have the benefit of deductible interest *as well as* no capital gains tax upon the sale of your home, the best tax advantages of both countries. Suddenly, Canadians utilizing The Smith Manoeuvre will have even larger financial advantages than their American cousins.

The fact that our American friends can deduct most of their mortgage interest when we can't goes some distance to explain why their standard of living is higher than ours in Canada.

A $200,000 house mortgage at 7% interest costs approximately $13,700 in interest during the first year, whether you live in Canada or the United States. The difference is that the American can claim the interest as deductible and, at a 40% marginal tax rate, he would receive a tax refund of $13,700 x .40 = $5,480. You, as a Canadian, may claim no tax refund. Unless you know how to do The Smith Manoeuvre.

The Canada Revenue Agency (CRA) is very strict about claims for deductibility of interest. This item bears repeating. The basic test for deductibility revolves around the answer to the question *'to what purpose did you put the money that you borrowed?'* If you borrowed to buy the family car, to take a vacation, to buy a cottage or your principal residence, then you may not claim the interest on the loan as a tax deduction. On the other hand, if you borrowed the money to invest, with a reasonable expectation of earning income from your investment, you may deduct the interest.

Interest and dividends from investments are acceptable forms of income for purposes of determining deductible interest claims, but capital gains are not. In the case of borrowing to invest in mutual funds and stock, the CRA allows the interest to be deductible even in the cases where a portion of the gain is likely to be capital gains. Your financial planner or your accountant will counsel you on this matter if he feels you are exposed in any way.

Some Canadians assume that if their house is the bank's security for a loan, then the interest is not tax deductible. This is important: the security offered for a loan has nothing to do with whether the interest expense is deductible. The main test is: *'what did you do with the money that you borrowed?'*

Some Canadians assume that conventional loans with blended payments that include both an interest and a principal reduction component are, by their nature, in the non-deductible category. This is also not true. Again, the type of loan, whether interest-only or blended payments, whether secured by your home or not, does not impact whether the interest is deductible. What matters is, *'to what purpose did you put the money that you borrowed?'*

The Next Time you Borrow

If the foregoing is making sense to you, it might be apparent that most Canadians and their bankers are getting their borrowing mechanics exactly backwards.

Imagine that a hard working and bright young lady has scrimped and saved to put together $30,000 of capital to invest in a business. Unfortunately, just as she is ready to buy her new business, her car blows up, and it becomes obvious that she also needs to borrow another $30,000 for a new family car. So she visits her friendly bank manager and asks for a $30,000 loan.

The bank manager is impressed. Usually people are coming to borrow money when they have no money, but this ambitious lady has $30,000 of her own. She looks like a good risk to him, so he smiles a big smile and says, "sit right down and I will write you up a car loan for $30,000."

And everybody is happy. Our heroine went in for a $30,000 loan and got it. The banker has made a low risk loan to a motivated young business lady. The carmaker has sold another car. And in the background, the taxman is smiling too because the way the loan was written up, the interest expense will not be tax deductible.

The loan was made backwards. A common but large mistake.

Our new business lady can be forgiven for making the mistake of asking for "a loan" instead of "an *investment* loan" because she was not taught the crucial difference between deductible interest (good interest) and non-deductible interest (bad interest) in her public school. Unless she subsequently went to business school, the odds are that she was not taught the difference at university or college either. Her parents and her relatives, her friends and her co-workers, plus her neighbours to the front, behind and next-door are likely all doing it wrong as well. They tend to make poor teachers regarding things financial. That's one reason financial planners were invented. If you don't have one you should consider getting one.

Very few Canadians understand the importance of differentiating between good debt and bad debt. In fact, very few Canadians know much about personal financial planning. It is written elsewhere that most Canadians spent more time last night watching TV than they have spent in their entire life learning about personal financial planning.

If I were the King of Canada, I would, as one of my first acts, decree that every year, starting with Grade One, part of the curriculum would be devoted to personal financial planning. The payoff for the students and the resultant payoff for Canada would be immense. Canadians would learn how to take care of their own financial well being rather than depending on failing corporate and government retirement programs.

But what about the banker?

Does the banker understand how important this distinction between good debt and bad debt really is? What should the banker have done when this woman came in to see him for her loan?

Instead of selling her a non-deductible interest loan for a car, he should instead have sold her a deductible-interest loan so she could invest the borrowed money into her new business. She would then be able to use her own $30,000 to pay cash for the car. That simple act, at no disadvantage to the bank, would have made the customer's interest expense a tax deduction.

He either knew, or should have known, that the difference to his customer was very important. If the loan interest rate was 6%, then the first year interest expense on the $30,000 loan would be about $1,800 dollars, regardless of whether the loan was for investment in her business or for the car. But if the loan was for the business, the $1,800 interest expense would be tax deductible. At the 40% tax bracket, our young entrepreneur would receive a $720 tax refund cheque, no charge, a gift, free, gratis, from the tax department.

That's a nice reward for simply writing up a loan one-way versus the other way.

But there's more.

Next year there will be another tax refund cheque, also free. And the year after that. In fact, if the loan was established as an interest-only loan, our business lady could still be getting free tax refund cheques for $720 every year until she retired at age 130.

If the bank manager knew, or should have known, that he could have provided a tax refund of such a magnitude to his customer simply by counseling her to borrow for the business purpose so she could use her own tax-paid funds to buy her car, and if the amount of interest the bank was getting for either type of loan was identical, why did he sell her the wrong loan?

You might guess that the bank would prefer to take the loan security of a car over the loan security of a new business, which is probably true. But nothing precludes the banker from taking the security of the car for the investment loan. The customer would be indifferent. If the banker had any reservations about the loan, he could even request the security of both the car and the new business. So the security for the loan is not the reason that the banker did not do this no-cost favour for the customer.

Perhaps the reason is simply because banks have always done it that way.

This simply shows that the educated borrower has a better chance for success in this life than does the uneducated borrower. You may feel you are getting too old to get educated, and if that's where you are, then retain a financial planner to analyze your situation. And let him/her deal with the banker on your behalf.

Conspiracy theorists will say that the Grey People in Government are colluding with the Grey People in the Banking Industry to keep the minions ignorant about the power of deductible interest. I think not. It's just plain old inertia at work. The lenders and the tax department don't care if you don't care. Not much has changed – if you want it done right, do it yourself – get involved – take charge.

By paying attention to the simple rule that you use borrowed money to make your investments, and you use your own tax-paid funds to buy your life style such as food, clothing, vacations, cars, toys, cottages and your home, you will be enormously ahead of your friends, neighbours and co-workers, as measured by your net worth.

Concerns

Now that we understand that there are two kinds of interest in Canada, deductible and non-deductible, we need to decide what to do about it.

Even if we can agree that good debt is better than bad debt, we have a few concerns.

1. We already happen to have a large debt in the form of a house mortgage, and we now know that the interest on a house mortgage is not deductible. It seems we are out of luck.

2. Even if we can see that good debt is better than bad debt, do we want to engage a strategy that is different from that which most others employ? Don't we at least need to be able to quantify the difference between the two methodologies?

3. While we overcame our dislike of debt at the moment we signed for that monster mortgage, we are now determined to get rid of that debt. The Canadian Dream is still alive – you want your mortgage paid off no later than the day you retire (Figure 5.1).

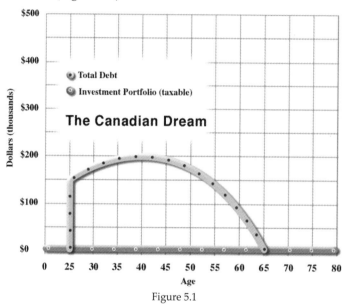

Figure 5.1

4. Most Canadians are working hard to get their mortgage paid off, fully intent that when that day comes, they will then be free to invest the former mortgage payment to build an investment portfolio. In our example in Figure 5.1, notice that this mortgage got paid off just in time to retire at age 65, but we are showing this homeowner as having no Investment Portfolio. He was able to

afford to handle his mortgage, but had nothing left with which to purchase investments.

5. Canadians can draw some comfort from the thought that if they don't have enough income in retirement, they will be able to get a reverse mortgage to generate cash flow by taking the equity from their newly paid off home. Based on the copious amount of advertising being done every day on TV and in the national papers, it is obvious that the Canadian Home Income Plan (CHIP) people see a big market developing for reverse mortgages.

Debt Paydown Versus Debt Conversion

Most ordinary Canadians have an aversion to debt. It probably stems from our earliest days when our grandparents admonished us that debt was bad, and that we should not borrow. Before income tax arrived in 1917, the advice of our grandparents was perhaps appropriate enough. The government was wise enough to recognize that businesses would be more likely to increase infrastructure and build inventories if the interest paid on money borrowed to grow the business was tax deductible. The wealthy people who ran the businesses extrapolated the strategy to their personal financial affairs through the advice of their tax lawyers and accountants. The businesses thrived and the wealthy prospered. The government increased its tax revenue from the growing businesses and the new employees who found work in the expanded economy.

Only the ordinary people did not participate in this wise tax measure. Being ordinary people meant they could not afford the expensive accountants and lawyers to give them advice. Being ordinary people, they felt fortunate they could even afford to service the large debt of their mortgage. Unfortunately, in Canada, the interest expense on the mortgage was not tax deductible. Businesses and wealthy people had a significant tax benefit by virtue of their wealth. They could afford expensive lawyers and accountants. The ordinary people were left with large, non-deductible debts, and consequently enjoyed no tax mitigation.

That's how it was, and that's how it is today. Stats Can tells us there are 10.5 million families in Canada, and about 3.5 million are carrying non-deductible mortgages.

Stats Can also provides statistics that indicate who is wealthy and who is not. The agency advises that 53% of the net worth of Canada is held by 10% of the population. We can represent this interesting statistic as The Wealth Pyramid, Figure 5.2. Let's assume that those people in the 10% category are the wealthy. It follows then that 90% of Canadians are in the not -wealthy category. It is in this 90% pool of Canadians where we will find almost all the non-deductible mortgages. People with non-deductible mortgages probably don't consider themselves wealthy – yet. Most probably assume that the wealthy have no mortgage. In fact many wealthy folks do have mortgages on their property, but usually they are mortgages that secure loans for other investments they control. As a result, the interest expenses of the mortgages of the wealthy tend to generate tax deductible interest. And yours doesn't. But it can. And it should.

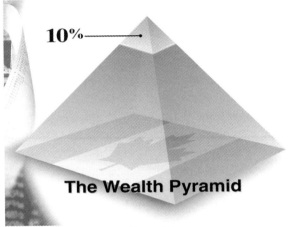

10% ————•

The Wealth Pyramid

Figure 5.2

Every once in a while, in an effort to get elected, some political party runs on a platform that offers deductible interest to get votes. If the USA can do it, then why not Canada? The main reason is that we have a larger country, with one-tenth the population all demanding the same high level of government services they have in the USA. We couldn't afford the tax hit.

The total conventional mortgage pool in Canada is about 500 billion dollars. At 6%, that would be 30 billion in tax deductions which would have to be made up by increasing taxes elsewhere, or decreasing services.

This would also give tax breaks to only the one third of Canadian families who had a mortgage, so it would discriminate against renters and those in paid-for homes.

The main reason it is bad politics is that it is a give-away program. There is little in the way of a quid-pro-quo for Canada.

The Smith Manoeuvre provides the home owner the free tax deductions plus an investment portfolio, and the government gets the benefit of the new investment which can be taxed. There are no losers. This is a true win-win scenario.

Let's Compare

It is difficult to alter the inertia of many generations passing financial messages down the line over the years. This is especially true when these messages are repeated and reinforced by some financial planners and industry gurus.

We need to compare the common sequential approach to debt and investment employed by nearly all mortgage holders in Canada against the promise of The Smith Manoeuvre.

Jack and Joe

Let's assume these two gentlemen have just turned 40, and have identical homes, families, mortgages, training, jobs and aspirations.

They each buy identical houses and both are destined to attain the Canadian Dream (Figure 5.1) which is to retire themselves and their mortgage on their 65th birthday.

Circumstances are such that they will manage to pay their mortgages off, but will not have had the means to gather any other assets to provide retirement income. That's why Figure 5.1 shows no investment portfolio. They are not too concerned because they know that they can always get a reverse mortgage at age 65 to augment their cash flow, because the house will be free and clear.

Jack First

Jack was on vacation and missed reading the book "*The Smith Manoeuvre*". He got a $200,000 mortgage at 7% and managed to pay it off right on schedule the day he retired. His company pension had failed a few years back and the CPP and OAS were being clawed back by the government. Jack had to resort to a reverse mortgage in order to have enough retirement income. The story of his life with mortgage debt is shown in Figure 5.3. Thank goodness the bank was there to give him what he needed. He borrowed $80,000, the maximum of 40% of the value of his appraisal, and the monthly annuity income was just enough to keep him comfortable until he died at 80. The major downside was that his house had no equity left in it. It was sold and the proceeds went to the bank to pay off the reverse mortgage loan, which was the contract. In actuality, Jack had been working for the bank from the time he took his first 100% leveraged house mortgage at age 25 until he died at age 80. The bank owned his house 100% at age 25 and again at age 80. In between he paid mortgage payments for 40 years of his life while he worked, with the bank holding his house as security. For the last 15 years of his life, no longer employed, he lived off the equity in his house that he had worked 40 years to make free and clear. It was only free and clear for one day – his 65th birthday, in this example.

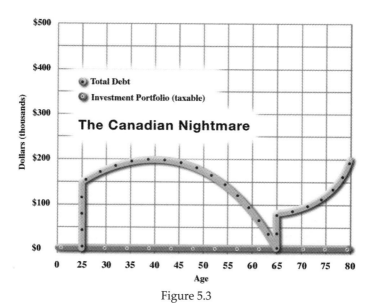

Figure 5.3

None of this is improper. Jack was grateful that the bank would lend him 100% of the money to buy his first house at age 25. Jack understood that he was really just renting the bank's money. He knew their job was to earn a return on the investment of their shareholders. He was grateful again at age 65 when they loaned him $80,000 even though he was unemployed. Yes, they took a premium on the rate, and the fees were stiff, but nobody else was on hand to help out. It's unreasonable to bash the banks for supplying cash when few others are willing or able. (If you want to get even with the banks, buy their shares. Own a piece of the banks – they are on to a good thing.)

Joe Bought the Book and the Calculator

And he's glad he did.

The first thing Joe learned was never to buy a fixed term mortgage. For the rest of his life he stayed short and saved thousands of dollars.

The most important thing Joe learned though was that it was possible and important to convert the bad debt he already owned into good debt. It did not matter that he had $200,000 worth of non-deductible debt, because using The Smith Manoeuvre, he would be able to convert it from bad debt to good debt. All Joe had to do was emulate methods used by business and by the wealthy, and he would grow his net worth by thousands and thousands of dollars. All he had to do was realize that in his blind determination to pay off his mortgage, he was choking off any hope he had to become financially independent. All he had to do was realize that the way to much improved net worth was not by reducing his debt, but rather by converting it from the bad kind to the good kind by leaving his debt constant at $200,000 during the conversion process. The objective is to follow the trail blazed by the wealthy and by businesses who learned a long time ago that you measure wealth by net worth, not by how little debt you have. Businesses and the wealthy carry *optimum* debt, not minimum debt and not maximum debt.

Joe learned that while the wealthy carry debt and leverage their net worth using Other People's Money (OPM), they rarely carry non-deductible debt. They convert bad debt to good debt as fast as possible. Joe's problem was that he did have debt, his house mortgage, but it was the wrong kind of debt. Joe needed to learn what the wealthy learned from their tax lawyers and their tax accountants – how to convert bad debt to good debt.

The Conversion Process

Figure 5.4 illustrates what Joe did to effect The Smith Manoeuvre. The line with the white dots shows the first mortgage (bad debt) being amortized. As fast as it drops, the equity is being re-borrowed at the same speed, represented by the line with the plus signs (good debt). This means the total of good and bad debt together will add to $200,000 at all times. The debt will remain level. This is represented by the line with the black dots.

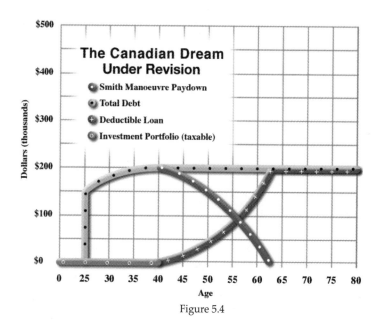

Figure 5.4

The assets being purchased each month will grow on a compounding basis of 10% per year in this example. The total of the investment portfolio (personal pension plan) at Joe's age 65 will have reached $509,000 represented by the line with the white circles.

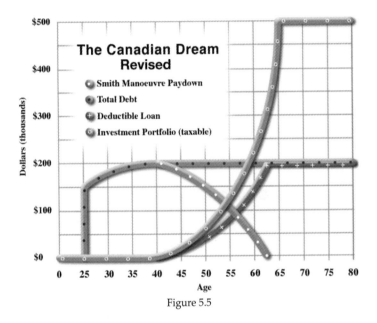

Figure 5.5

The portfolio total is shown to stay flat at $509,000 from age 65 to 80 because the assumption is that Joe will convert the portfolio to income production, perhaps dividends, at age 65 when he retires. The portfolio is providing Joe's supplementary retirement income. Jack had to get a reverse mortgage. Joe has the income from $509,000 to live on; Jack has the income on only $80,000. Part of Joe's income would be needed to service the interest on the $200,000 investment loan which continues to exist.

All Joe had to do to pick up these advantages was to come to understand that he was far further ahead to drop his plan of trying to pay off his mortgage. Instead, as fast as he reduced his mortgage each month, all he had to do was borrow back the same amount to buy more investments for his portfolio. His debt would not increase – it would remain constant.

Joe reckoned that if he could handle his $200,000 mortgage today, it would become ever easier to handle as the years progressed. By being willing to hold his debt flat at the level from where it started, Joe was able to benefit more and more each year from the compounding growth of his portfolio. As well, the increasing tax refund cheque he was getting each year allowed him to make extra payments against his mortgage, which new equity was also instantly re-borrowed to increase the portfolio yet again.

Joe made these large improvements without leveraging. As we have seen, leveraging is described as increasing your debt by borrowing to invest. Part of the risk in leveraging comes from the increased costs of carrying the higher debt. If your debt does not increase, you are not leveraging. The Smith Manoeuvre is not a leveraging program because even though you will be borrowing to purchase investments, you will not have access to the funds unless first you reduce your mortgage by the amount you wish to borrow to invest. If you reduce your bad debt before you borrow back to invest, you have not leveraged, you have *converted*. The difference is important to understand.

In truth the leveraging occurred earlier when Joe borrowed $200,000 to buy his house. In fact he leveraged 100% into a bad debt for a good purchase, his house. With The Smith Manoeuvre available for his use, Joe can now make a prior good decision (to leverage into a house) into a near-perfect decision (to convert the bad debt into good debt).

Using The Smith Manoeuvre, Joe has managed to improve his net worth in dramatic fashion without increasing his debt, and without using any of his own cash flow. In fact, Joe has a new source of free cash flow. It is courtesy of the tax department when he claims the fruits of the conversion of bad debt to good debt – free tax refund cheques.

There is another rarely understood strategy available to Joe that provides him an advantage without cost. It is called capitalization of interest.

Capitalization

Suppose you have a loan for $10,000 and the interest for the current month of $100 is due. You could open your wallet and turn over the $100 to the lender to pay the rent on the loan. If you have cash flow problems, you might be able to convince the lender to add the interest expense to the principal owed so that now you owe the lender $10,100.

This procedure is called capitalizing the interest – the interest has been converted to capital. Next month you will have to pay interest on $10,100.

Banks don't usually like to capitalize consumer debt – they would prefer at the least to be receiving monthly interest, in which case the principal would stay constant, but interest would not accumulate. Many loans, such as mortgages and term loans are set up as amortizing loans where a monthly payment covers the interest expense for the month, plus an amount that reduces the principal of the loan. When the banker capitalizes interest, he is simply lending you more money.

If the mortgage you have is not generating tax deductible interest, you might as well pay the interest with your tax-paid income. Capitalization provides no advantages when you are dealing with non-deductible debt. But if your loan is for investment and the interest is tax deductible, then you can pick up an advantage by capitalizing the interest.

The CRA specifically advises in Section 20(1)(c) that if interest on a loan is deductible, then so is the interest on the interest. In other words, compound interest on deductible loans is deductible. The rule to follow is this – as long as you still have any non-deductible debt such as your mortgage, capitalize the interest on deductible debt so that your tax-paid cash flow can be used to overpay your bad-debt mortgage faster. Divert every tax paid dollar you can find against your first mortgage – don't use your cash to pay for investments or to pay deductible interest – these items should be paid with borrowed money.

Two things happen:

1. Your mortgage drops faster so you will be able to invest for more years after it is paid off.
2. If your mortgage drops faster, then your investment loan rises faster which means your tax deductions are bigger sooner. This is good news when you are referencing tax refund cheques.

When finally all your bad debt has been converted to good debt, there is no remaining reason to continue to capitalize the interest. On the day your bad-debt mortgage has finally been converted completely to a good-interest investment loan, you will no longer have to make the monthly payment on your first mortgage. Instead you will be able to invest that amount, minus the amount it takes to service the interest expense (deductible) on your investment loan.

If you insist on starting to pay off the good-debt investment loan two unnecessary bad things happen.

1. Your tax deductions which have now reached a maximum will begin to drop as the loan reduces.
2. More importantly, if you are using cash flow to reduce a loan (a good loan) then by definition your cash is not available to buy investments for your portfolio. Financially you are far better off to maintain the good loan at its original level, service the monthly interest and continue to increase your investment portfolio. To be so debt adverse that you would start to pay off this good loan is very expensive for your future net worth. Some people are so debt adverse that they don't care how much it costs to pay down the debt. But the choice is yours to make.

Money for Capitalization Comes From Somewhere

We have insisted that the elements of The Smith Manoeuvre require no new cash from you, and as well, you do not need to increase your debt. This is true. In fact, as you have seen, The Smith Manoeuvre actually generates free new cash flow for your family every year into the future, courtesy of the tax department.

You will be doing your best to divert all kinds of cash from all kinds of sources as extra payments against your mortgage. The funds that come as tax refunds, raises, bonuses, gifts, lottery winnings, dividends, capital gains and inheritances can serve no greater purpose than to reduce your bad-debt mortgage. You know there are multiple rewards. Not only does your mortgage go down faster, but you know you will turn around and re-borrow the same amounts in order to purchase more investments for your portfolio.

But let's say there were no extra monies of any kind that could be applied. Where do you get the cash to allow the borrowing room you need to have to let the bank increase the investment loan to fund the amount of interest being capitalized?

The answer is, from the monthly principal reduction that occurs each month when the monthly mortgage payment is applied.

Up to this point, we have been indicating that the portion of your monthly mortgage payment that actually reduces the principal of the loan is immediately borrowed back to invest. In fact, in order to be able to claim that The Smith Manoeuvre requires no incremental cash from you, what really happens is this: the amount of investment credit freed up when the mortgage payment is made will be used first to provide room to capitalize the interest on the deductible loan. The remainder of the credit available will then be used to purchase investments.

If your payment on your first mortgage is $1,000 of which $800 is interest to the bank, and $200 reduces your loan, then you can borrow $200 to invest. But first we have to pay, say $20 interest (deductible) on our investment loan. The amount we have left is $180 which we use to buy investments.

In this fashion we can truly continue to say that The Smith Manoeuvre requires no new cash from you, and as well, you don't have to increase your debt. The debt will stay level while the conversion proceeds over the months ahead.

My Bank Doesn't Want to Capitalize

They probably won't. But a financial revolution has been taking place. Partly because of foreign competition but mostly because ordinary people are using the Internet to get educated, things are changing rapidly. So the big banks may initially be reluctant to capitalize for you, but as more people like you request these services, they will begin to co-operate. This is because they will start losing their mortgages to other banks and credit unions like VanCity and Coast Capital who do capitalize. They will eventually come around. It is called competition and free enterprise. The market is very powerful. If you are rejected by your bank for capitalization privileges, shop around for other more caring institutions, such as the credit unions. In the alternative, retain a financial planner who offers assistance with The Smith Manoeuvre.

If you and your planner are unable to find any institution in your area that will capitalize, implement The Smith Manoeuvre without the capitalization feature. You will be able to enjoy capitalization later because sooner or later, this service will undoubtedly be common practice in your locale.

Guerrilla Capitalization

If you and your advisor are determined, you can effect capitalization in the following manner without the direct assistance of the bank. This move requires two banks or two accounts at the same bank. This is a guerrilla style personal financing strategy.

1. Set up standard Smith Manoeuvre banking arrangements at a bank or credit union.
2. If the institution refuses to offer capitalization services, open a small creditline at the same bank or a different bank, for, say, $5,000.
3. When your deductible interest creditline statement arrives indicating you owe, say, $200 interest for the month, ask the bank to capitalize the interest for you.
4. If they won't, borrow $200 from your $5,000 creditline at the same bank or a different bank and pay the interest expense.
5. Do this every month until you have borrowed, say, $4,000 of interest from the $5,000 creditline.
6. Now borrow $4,000 from your main deductible interest creditline and pay the $5,000 creditline back down to zero and start again.
7. The interest on both the $5,000 creditline and your main investment line is tax deductible because proceeds were transferred back and forth between

two credit facilities that were themselves for investment purposes or for paying tax-deductible interest. As per section 20(1)(c), compounding interest on deductible loans is itself deductible.

8. It is this knowledge that the banks have but don't explain to ordinary people that will lead them to agree that they might as well just offer capitalization services. This is because I've shown you how to do it with or without their help.

Caution: You must never use either of these deductible interest investment lines to purchase anything that is not an investment, as it might disqualify your claim for deductible interest.

If you discover a mistake, reverse the error, preferably with the help of a planner, including the reversal of any and all compound interest on the tainted capital. Document the account activity in detail and keep copies of the applicable cheques and bank statements for the review of the taxman who will almost certainly reassess you if your records are not in order. And that's fair enough, in my opinion.

In the same vein, you need to realize that if you purchase an investment with borrowed money and claim the interest as a tax deduction, the CRA is very strict on the rule that that asset always be in your possession if you continue to claim the interest deduction. No asset, no deduction, unless you sell an asset and immediately repurchase a new qualifying asset to take its place. It is not as simple as this, so once more you are advised to get help from your planner who is quite aware of what precautions you need to take to stay onside with Mr. Taxman.

One last caution. Some planners (poor planners) in the past have recommended that you borrow to buy an asset, claim the deductible interest, then contribute the asset to the RRSP to claim another tax benefit. Just so you know, the tax department assumes you have sold that asset the moment you put it into the RRSP, and as previously indicated, that portion of the loan invested in the transferred asset will have its applicable interest expense disqualified from being deductible from that moment forward.

You may transfer assets that were purchased with borrowed money to an RRSP but the interest expense will cease to be deductible. Keep great records, just in case.

This chapter will be somewhat mystifying to some readers no doubt. If this were easy, everybody would already be doing it. So, while it may be a bit daunting for some, the hope is that you will persevere to get a basic grounding in why it is important for you to convert your bad debt to good debt now rather than later.

If you are really keen on understanding the details of interest deductibility you might want to slog through the CRA bulletin on this topic. Just Google for IT533.

You now understand that good debt is much, much better for you than bad debt. Your problem seems insurmountable because you already have a lot of debt in your house mortgage and it's the bad kind.

Is it too late for you?

6

IMPLEMENTATION

The Smith Manoeuvre is egalitarian. It is going to provide a service to anyone in Canada who has a conventional mortgage on his or her home, with some modest exceptions. Ordinary Canadians using The Smith Manoeuvre will be able to deduct the interest expense of their mortgages, a privilege ordinarily reserved for the wealthy, who can afford high priced lawyers and accountants to show them how it's done.

That being said, there are some mortgages that will be delayed in their implementation of The Smith Manoeuvre. It will be too soon for you if the bank thinks your debt service ratio is too high. You may find resistance if you are a farm or hobby farm. You may also find the lending value reduced to a maximum of 60% of value if you are not inside "town limits".

To this point in the book, the examples have been given for a family with a 75% mortgage. These are commonly referred to as conventional mortgages. If you need to borrow more than 75%, the bank classifies your loan as a high-ratio mortgage. They require that you pay for insurance from CMHC or GE who guarantee to pay off your mortgage should you default.

This is a fair reaction from the lenders who need to insure themselves if they take on increased risk. The incremental expense to the homeowner is more than offset by advantages of home ownership.

There is nothing to prevent you from operating The Smith Manoeuvre on a high-ratio mortgage. If you have a 90% high-ratio mortgage, you can institute The Smith Manoeuvre if you can convince your lender to provide you a matching 90% readvanceable creditline. If your banker won't provide that facility, you may wish to ask your financial planner to move your mortgage to a different institution who will give you the services you require.

Some institutions now offer 100% high ratio mortgages, and it is probable that they will eventually get around to offering matching 100% readvanceable facilities so that The Smith Manoeuvre can be employed at any mortgage ratio.

There are strategies to follow if you wish to get down to the 75% level to avoid the additional cost of a high ratio mortgage.

1. Sell some assets and apply the proceeds against the mortgage.
2. Borrow enough to pay the first mortgage down to the 75% level. The banker you are approaching to set up The Smith Manoeuvre will usually be happy to lend you funds on a secured or unsecured basis if you are then going to pay down your first mortgage with the proceeds. This "borrowing from Peter to pay Paul" is usually a bad scene, but the banker is apt to feel differently if the new funds allow you to start up The Smith Manoeuvre program.

You may also be delayed if you currently have more than one mortgage on your property. A good financial planner or an interested and motivated banker will usually be able to make it work as long as the two mortgages (or even three) don't exceed 75% of the value of the home. In fact, the real live client case to follow had two prior mortgages. It was the VanCity manager, Greg Duncan, who suggested a great solution.

If you experience any resistance from a banker, consider working with a financial planner who in turn works with a mortgage broker. A mortgage broker can do magic in solving marginal situations that are not straight forward for a conventional banker. A good mortgage broker who understands The Smith Manoeuvre will be able to get you correctly financed to get the most out of your situation. More and more financial planners are teaming up with mortgage brokers to the benefit of all, especially you.

The home owners in Brampton and Mississauga are well served in this fashion by the team of Ed Rempel, financial planner and Dorothy Lazzari, a TD Canada Trust mortgage specialist. They jointly conduct evening seminars on The Smith Manoeuvre once or twice a month. Attendance varies from 30 to 60 people per session which means they are meeting a lot of mortgages that need converting.

The Whites Do The Smith Manoeuvre

Perhaps the easiest way to illustrate the steps your financial planner will take to establish The Smith Manoeuvre for your family is to utilize the documents exchanged with VanCity in a real live case.

Following are the pertinent rounded statistics on real live clients whom we will call Jim and Brenda White. This young couple work hard in the hospitality industry – Jim is a chef and Brenda is a receptionist

50,000	joint income
184,000	appraised house value
129,000	total of 1st and 2nd BNS mortgages
88,000	term deposits, GIC's, currency
12,000	Mazda truck – 1994
162,000	net worth

On June 4th, I faxed a financing proposal to Greg Duncan at VanCity on behalf of the Whites (Figures 6.1.1 and 6.1.2). On June 7th, Greg Duncan faxed back his approval (Figure 6.2). (Notice the 3 day turn-around time.) He included a suggestion that the Whites would be further ahead to let VanCity payout both Bank of Nova Scotia (BNS) mortgages, even with a prepayment penalty to the BNS. And he was correct.

The Whites subsequently began investing by automatic withdrawal from their VanCity deductible investment creditline at the rate of $800 per month, and have not missed a month since.

The figure of $800 represents the approximate monthly reduction of the principal of the first mortgage. If the first is dropping at about $800 per month, the Whites want to ensure they invest the same amount by borrowing from their new investment line of credit. The interest expense on their new investment loan will be a tax deduction. The investment loan will increase at the same speed as the

Smith Consulting Group Ltd.

June 4, 2001

VanCity   By Fax: 595-5133
3055A Scott Street
Victoria, B.C.   V8R 4J9

Attention: Mr. Greg Duncan & Ms. Bev Shingles

Dear Greg & Bev,

_____ is the chef at _____, and _____ runs the front desk at the _____. They wish to set up the Smith Manoeuvre in order to convert their mortgage to tax deductible interest.

Income

$28,704
_21,696_
$50,400

Background

The _____ bought a house a year ago and assumed the vendors 6.05% BNS first and took a $44,700 BNS second. They made a $45,000 down payment, and have been overpaying the mortgages ever since. They have an unused $6,000 BNS credit line, and a VISA card that they payout each month. They have no debt other than the two mortgages.

The term of the BNS first matured today, and at our suggestion, the _____ have renewed it as an open mortgage. (The BNS 2nd has another 2 years on its term.)

Values

		$180,000	estimated value
	x .75%	135,000	lending value
	88,900		BNS 1st
	_40,000_		BNS 2nd
less:	$128,900	_128,900_	prior mortgages
		$ 6,100	available credit

Handwritten annotations:
ACTUAL
184,000 appraisal.
x.75 138,000 lending value
- 126,865 BNS
$ 11,135 avail credit
+25 K line

Re-Financing

Subject to confirmation of the appraisal value, our request is that VanCity supply a readvanceable mortgage for $135,000 being 75% of the property value, plus a $25,000 unsecured line of credit.

Figure 6.1.1

Use of Proceeds

The readvanceable will be used to payout the current BNS open first mortgage. The current BNS second mortgage will automatically move into first position.

The readvanceable will be set up in two segments. Segment A will be an open line of credit, non-deductible, which will be paid down very rapidly, and will be the amount needed to pay out the BNS first.

Segment B will be the deductible interest credit line to be used for investment purposes only, and will capitalize the interest monthly.

The BNS $6,000 credit line will be maintained as an unused emergency account.

The $25,000 unsecured credit line will be used to purchase . Please arrange servicing of this credit line at interest only, to be paid automatically each month from Segment B of the readvanceable.

Debt Service Ratio

$ 465	$ 6,000	BNS C/L, if drawn	p+1.5
4,236	40,000	BNS second mortgage, $353/mth	7.45%
1,408		property tax	
6,445	88,900	VanCity – Segment A readvanceable	p+1
442	6,100	VanCity – Segment B readvanceable	p+1
1,938	25,000	VanCity – unsecured C/L	P+1.5
$14,934			

$$\frac{\text{debt service}}{\text{income}} \quad \frac{14,934}{50,400} = 29.63\%$$

I look forward to hearing from you.

Yours truly,
SMITH CONSULTING GROUP LTD.

Fraser Smith
President

/leo
enclosure

Figure 6.1.2

June 7, 20001

KittyHawk Securities Ltd.
Attention: Fraser Smith

Re:

New First and Second Mortgages--.

Dear Fraser:

We are prepared to approve the following mortgage and unsecured creditline package:

1) Conventional First mortgage of +/- 75% of A.A.C.I. appraised value @ Prime + 0% (Homeprime) to payout and discharge the existing Bank of Nova Scotia first mortgage of +/- $88,900.00 and Bank of Nova Scotia Second mortgage of +/- $40,000.00 plus penalty. The payment will be based on a 25 yr. amortization.

2) Re-advanceable Second Mortgage Creditline mortgage up to 75% L.T.V., at Prime + 0% with payments to capitalize within the limit (Z1).

3) Unsecured $25,000.00 Creditline (Z2) at Prime plus 1.5% with interest payments to be paid monthly from the second mortgage creditline. Any loan interest due that exceeds authorized lending limits is to be paid by the borrowers on demand.

Please have the   contact Bev at 519-7424 to book an appointment to sign our internal documents, prior to their appointment at Bob Adair's office to sign mortgage documents.

Yours truly,
Vancouver City Savings Credit Union

Greg Duncan
Manager

Figure 6.2

mortgage loan drops, thus their debt will stay level – it will not increase.

The Whites also cashed the liquid assets they owned, thus reducing their mortgage. Some of their GIC's will mature in the years ahead and will be applied against the mortgage. The pay downs will immediately be re-borrowed to invest. Within a year their debt was down to $103,000 from $128,000.

It seems almost certain, based on their current progress, that the Whites should be finished with their bad-debt mortgage in less than five years. Their debt should stay constant, good debt and bad debt combined, at around $155,000. The interest, in less than five years, should be totally deductible at 7%, tax deductions would start immediately, rising each year until conversion was complete. In the 5th year, and for every year thereafter, there would be tax deductions of $10,850, as long as the loan was kept in place.

Because they very clearly understand the benefit of deductible versus non-deductible interest, the odds are very high that Brenda and Jim will still be collecting an annual tax deduction of $10,850 the year that they reach 130 years of age. Why would they ever use cash to pay off a tax-deductible loan? Better they should use that cash instead to pick up even more investments. Or maybe some of that cash could be used to increase their life style. Their choice.

Most banks, credit unions, trust companies and some life insurance companies have some variation on the readvanceable line of credit. Manulife has a very interesting product, which can be easily adopted to accommodate The Smith Manoeuvre. It is called *Manulife One*, and you can read about it at _www.manulifeone.com_. This financial offering looks excellent, and I predict that most institutions will have to offer similar programs as this instrument catches on. It is very popular in Australia.

If I were you, I would use a financial planner to assist. You will need the following information for the planner and the new banks you are approaching.

1. The usual questionnaire regarding address, phone, employer, years at current address, etc.
2. Proof of income. The income page from your tax returns or your recent pay stubs will do the trick.
3. A statement of net worth – assets and liabilities, which will indicate loans and payments.
4. You will likely need a recent statement regarding your current mortgage, and details regarding property tax. RRSP statements are an advantage.

The bank will do a credit check too. The fact that you are making arrangements to *convert* your debt as opposed to increasing it makes the decision easier for the bank. You are not asking to increase your credit, you are asking for rearrangements that will allow you to *convert* your credit. This will not be a hard decision for the banker in almost all cases. The fact that you have already qualified for a mortgage is great comfort to the banker. So go get 'em!

Subsequent Account Adjustments

In the case of the Whites, you will notice on the first page of my proposal that if the house appraised at our estimate of $180,000, then there would be $6,100 available credit, for investment purposes. As it turned out, the house appraised at $184,000, so we re-submitted the adjusted proposal as follows:

	$184,000	appraised value
x .75	138,000	lending value – 75%
less	126,865	payout both BNS mortgages
	11,135	available credit

(I suggested to the Whites that they use some cash on hand to reduce the BNS second mortgage *prior* to calculating the three-month interest penalty for early payout, so the actual payout was less than the original proposal.)

VanCity has agreed to lend a maximum of 75% of the appraised value of the prior mortgages. In this case, there is one prior VanCity mortgage of $126,865 (which used to be two prior mortgages at BNS). The rule VanCity will follow for the time being is that they will give the Whites an investment creditline of 75% of $184,000 *minus* $126,865 being the prior first mortgage amount at inception. The Authorized Limit of $11,135 is available now to borrow for investment purposes. The interest expense on the investment loan will be a tax deduction.

Because the total debt came in at $126,865 after the reorganization we should recognize a truism at this point. While there is $11,135 of available credit that can be invested, if we use it, we will be leveraging $11,135. We are going to convert $126,865 of bad debt to good debt so no leveraging is occurring there because the debt will stay at the same level. If we use any of the $11,135 that is available, we will be leveraging. In the Whites' case, leveraging $11,135 was totally appropriate and suitable for them, so we did.

The first regular payment against the first mortgage will reduce the amount of the first mortgage principal. In addition, the Whites might take advantage of early payment provisions and make a lump sum reduction of the first mortgage. While the new equity generated is theoretically available to be re-borrowed, in practise, you will wait some months before you submit a request to recalculate a new, larger "Authorized Limit". The Whites would at least wait until they had nearly used up their investment creditline of $11,135.

To increase the "Authorized Limit", a written request is emailed to Greg Duncan or Bev Collison at VanCity requesting a re-advance. VanCity confirms the current reduced amount of the first mortgage, subtracts that number from the 75% lending value, and the result is the new higher "Authorized Limit". If the first mortgage had gone down $5,000 since inception of the credit facility, then the "Authorized Limit" would increase by $5,000. This would allow the Whites several more months of investing at their predetermined rate of $800 per month.

When a re-advance is approved, the Whites are asked to sign a new Creditline Mortgage Agreement for the higher amount.

The re-advance process will continue every few months as needed, until the first mortgage has been paid off.

If the first mortgage were at a different institution, the Whites would need to obtain proof of the current first mortgage balance for VanCity's files.

Several banks are now offering readvanceable mortgages that automatically increase the limit of the investment creditline each time the first mortgage is reduced. This reduction is going to happen each time a mortgage payment is applied on the first mortgage. It is very convenient when the resulting equity is automatically transferred to increase the borrowing limit on your investment creditline. This happens on First Line's Matrix Mortgage and BMO's ReadiLine to name a few. And that's about it. Not so bad. It is a rather simple process actually, and it soon becomes a routine. But the magic of deductible interest is enhanced as each month goes by, and the results are predictable and exciting. It is truly worth the effort.

The Ten Steps of Implementation

The following steps are for the case where the client wishes to avoid a high ratio mortgage. Accordingly, mortgaging is capped at 75% of appraised value.

Step 1   Your financial planner will find a banker who will agree to provide you Smith Manoeuvre facilities, subject to a written proposal and subject to an appraisal of the value of your home.

Step 2   Your planner will present your proposal to the banker, built on the best guess he/she can make as to the value of your home, to be subsequently verified by an appraisal. He or she will be requesting a readvanceable creditline, for 75% of the value of the appraisal, secured by a mortgage on your home. Loan proceeds may be used to purchase investments.

Step 3   As soon as you are approved, subject to an appraisal, your planner will order the appraisal from a list of acceptable appraisers that the bank will provide.

Step 4   When the appraisal has been done, it will go to the banker along with a revised proposal illustrating the adjusted request for your readvanceable creditline which will be for 75% of the appraised value of your home as indicated by the appraisal.

Step 5   When approval has been provided, the banker will recommend a lawyer, or perhaps your planner has one that is acceptable to the bank, where the new readvanceable creditline mortgage will be prepared for your signature.

Step 6   You will receive new chequebooks for your new investment creditline, and begin building an investment portfolio. Every few months, as you reduce the first mortgage, you will borrow back to invest.

Step 7   When your investment borrowings start to approach the "Authorized Limit" of your investment creditline, your planner will provide the bank a written request to re-advance the limit.

Step 8   Sell any paid up assets you may own such as term deposits, CSB's, GIC's, mutual funds, stocks, bonds, and real estate and apply the proceeds against your first mortgage. Your planner or accountant will calculate any capital gains triggered by the sale so you can determine your reserve for taxes. Re-advance the investment creditline and re-borrow to replace tomorrow the assets you sold today. Use The Smithman Calculator, (check box III), to see what this little move does for your future net worth. You will be surprised at the positive lift a debt swap provides to your net worth.

Step 9   Stop buying term deposits, CSB's, GIC's, mutual funds, stocks, bonds and real estate with your pay cheque. Instead, divert the funds you ordinarily would spend on these items, against your first mortgage. Then borrow the same amount of funds back again and purchase the intended investments with borrowed money. (This is check box IV in The Smithman Calculator.)

Step 10 When you get your tax refund, be wise and pay this found money down against your first mortgage, then re-borrow the same amount and buy replacement investments.

You are on your way!

7

ACCELERATOR - THE CASH FLOW DAM

Cash Flow Dam I – Proprietors and Partners

There is a rather large group of Canadians running small businesses on an unincorporated basis, who also have a mortgage on their home. Ordinary Canadians, as well as these small business families are all able to enjoy free tax deductions and rapidly growing investment portfolios simply by implementing The Smith Manoeuvre. To also own an unincorporated business of any kind brings significant increased financial opportunity to this group of entrepreneurs.

When most small businesses get started, part of the excitement is going to the bank to open a business account. You order company chequebooks and deposit books. The money starts to flow in to your new bank account and at the end of the month you pay the company bills. If there is anything left, you write a cheque to yourself, call it draw, and deposit it to your personal chequing account.

If you don't have a house mortgage this is a fine and efficient setup. But if you do have a mortgage (or other non-deductible debt), then there is a much better way to structure your banking. It is called the Cash Flow Dam and it is so little known that Google can't find it.

Rationale

We will rely on the tax fact that money borrowed personally to invest in a business in order to generate income gives rise to deductible interest on that loan. The interest expense on the house mortgage is not deductible.

Further, nothing in the tax act says that you have to pay company expenses with revenue generated by the unincorporated business.

Being unincorporated means that for tax purposes, you and your company are the same person. Your accountant will total your annual company revenues, subtract company expenses and the difference, the profit, will be added to your other personal income for the calendar year.

The Smith Manoeuvre increases in power if the first mortgage can be paid down faster. This is because of the increased efficiency of your mortgage payment as discovered in Chapter 3. That will obviously happen if we can divert a portion of the revenue stream from your business against the first mortgage on your principal residence. The Cash Flow Dam makes that happen.

The amount of cash available from the company to apply against the first mortgage monthly will be an amount equal to the expenses of the company for the month. (Note that your monthly draw is not classified as an expense of the company.) Capital expenses as well as operating expenses qualify for the tax-deductible interest treatment if this expense is paid with borrowed money from your Smith Manoeuvre investment account.

Mechanics

1. At the end of each payables interval, tally all qualifying expense in the company. Keep good records each month. Be precise.

2. Write a cheque against your Smith Manoeuvre investment line of credit for the same amount, notate it *"Company Expenses"* and make it payable to your company. Pay the expenses with this money.

3. Write a company cheque payable to yourself for the total amount of the expenses. Notate it as *"Draw – re: expenses"*.

4. Deposit the cheque into your personal chequing account. From there, pay down your first mortgage by the same amount. This will be a lump sum payment in addition to your regular monthly payment. If your bank won't accept lump sum overpayments put the money in a separate savings account until you are eligible to make an overpayment. (Another reason to avoid fixed rate mortgages.)

Payoff

Using The Smithman Calculator example in Figure 3.2. we determined that a Canadian family, The Blacks, doing The Plain Jane version of The Smith Manoeuvre would reduce their tax bill by $41,980, knock 2.75 years of their 25-year mortgage and have an investment portfolio of $309,882, net of the investment loan. This assumes investments grow at an average of 10% per year, which is the average annual growth of the TSE for over 50 years. No resources are required from the family to effect this result. The portfolio may be taxable if liquidated.

If perchance the Blacks also had an unincorporated business, the value of The Smith Manoeuvre leaps ahead if the Cash Flow Dam strategy is employed. Figure 7.1 shows an example of the tax saved/reinvested, the years knocked off the mortgage, and the increased net worth for The Blacks in two cases. One is a very small company, which averages expenses of only $2,000 per month. The second example is a larger company with expenses of $10,000 per month.

	A	B	C
	Figure 3.2 Plain Jane	Expenses of $2,000 per month	Expenses of $10,000 per month
Taxes saved at 40%	$41,980	$87,270	$96,687
Years saved	2.75	19.17	23.42
Net worth improvement	$309,882	$718,927	$919,249

Figure 7.1

Combining the Plain Jane Smith Manoeuvre with the cash flow from your home business is worth over $700,000 in improved net worth in example B and over $900,000 for a larger business. These excellent numbers come from reorganizing the route your money takes. Reorganization does it. It is simple to do, and it is very profitable.

Cash Flow Dam II - House Rentals

Statistics Canada advises us that of the 10.5 million families in Canada, about 3.5 million live in rental accommodations. A large portion of the rental property industry is operated on an unincorporated basis by families who have decided to get into the business of supplying a home for someone else. They have an unincorporated rental business. Any of these entrepreneurs who also have a mortgage on their own home may enjoy free tax deductions and rapidly growing investment portfolios simply by implementing The Smith Manoeuvre, and they should. But if they also own a second house or apartment that they rent to others, they are entitled to a significant and incremental financial opportunity that costs them not much more than the time it takes to reorganize their financing.

Figure 7.2 provides an example of the incremental net worth your family would enjoy in two separate cases. Column B shows that if you were renting a condo out to somebody for $1,000 per month and if that just happened to also be the monthly cost to pay for the condo, your Smith Manoeuvre net worth would double from $309,000 to $613,000. If you were operating a four-plex at $5,000 per month, your net worth improvement would jump to $828,000. These increases in your net worth are free to you, and are in addition to the capital gain you expect to enjoy when someday you sell your revenue house.

	A	B	C
	Figure 3.2 Plain Jane	Expenses of $1,000 per month	Expenses of $5,000 per month
Taxes saved at 40%	$41,980	$79,598	$93,919
Years saved	2.75	16.00	22.08
Net worth improvement	$309,882	$613,197	$828,046

Figure 7.2

Where Does the Lift Come From?

It is obvious that the expense money and the revenue money are simply going in a circle each month, so how can this strategy improve your net worth?

The answer lies in the magic of compounding. The results are calculated by comparing the difference in family net worth between two strategies 25 years from today. The ending point where we do the comparison is the amortization period for your house mortgage, 25 years in this example.

The act of running cash flow from the business or the rental property in a circle through your personal accounts and your mortgage increases the efficiency of each subsequent mortgage payment.

We will use the example of the homeowners in Column B of Figure 7.2. They are doing The Smith Manoeuvre on their personal $200,000 mortgage, and now wish to use The Cash Flow Dam for their $1,000 per month rental property to accelerate The Smith Manoeuvre.

The conversion period rendered in Column B of Figure 7.2 shows that the 25 year mortgage we had on our principal residence will be paid out in 9.0 years because we have knocked 16.0 years off our mortgage. The Blacks were planning on making mortgage payments for 25 years at $1,400.83. If the debt has been converted to deductible debt in 9.0 years because of The Smith Manoeuvre plus the accelerator of the Cash Flow Dam, then $1,400.83 is available to put to work for the 16.0 years that remain to get to the end of the 25ᵗʰ year. This is how we are able to compare the Blacks' way to The Smith Manoeuvre way.

First Lift

Assume we have just completed the conversion of the first mortgage after only 9.0 years, in this example. The first use of the former monthly mortgage payment of $1,400.83 will be to pay the monthly interest expense on the $200,000 investment loan. This interest expense will be tax deductible. $200,000 at 5% in our example delivers tax deductions of $10,000 per year for 16.0 years. At our marginal tax rate of 40%, the tax refund will be $4,000 per year which will be immediately invested to compound as received each year. This provides our first lift, free, courtesy of the tax department.

Second Lift

Monthly interest expense on our $200,000 investment loan at 5% is $10,000 per year, is $833.73 per month. Our monthly payment is $1,400.83. Subtracting interest of $833.33 means we will have $567.50 per month left over to increase and compound our investment portfolio every month for the next 16.0 years. This provides the second lift.

The joint benefits in the example of Column B of Figure 7.2 total $613,197. Subtracting the $309,882 provided by Plain Jane confirms that the benefit provided by rotating the monthly revenue house rent money through the mortgage on the principal residence each month adds $303,315 to the family net worth. There are other accelerators to be utilized in similar fashion to be discussed in a future update of this book.

These calculations are done instantly for any mortgage and any assumption by The Smithman Calculator.

If you do have a profit, you would obviously benefit greatly if you used it to overpay your first mortgage, but don't forget to reserve for income tax on that profit.

Summary

The basic Plain Jane version of The Smith Manoeuvre gives this average family with a $200,000 mortgage an improvement of more than $300,000 in their net worth. Adding the little known strategy of the Cash Flow Dam doubles and nearly triples the already spectacular benefits of The Smith Manoeuvre for the Blacks in these two examples.

The Cash Flow Dam requires no new money and no new resources of any kind from the taxpayer. The benefits are free, and accrue as a result of reorganizing finances, just like wealthy people do.

The Cash Flow Dam does not work for incorporated companies because unlike unincorporated companies, the company is essentially considered another person for tax purposes. I can do no better than to once again suggest that you do yourself a disservice if you do not seek the advice of a financial planner or an accountant who is familiar with The Smith Manoeuvre.

My special thanks to Brian Dougherty, CA and Paul Winstanley, CA who taught me the Cash Flow Dam. Brian has been my beleaguered accountant for about a quarter of a century. He's an old guy.

8

WHAT'S IN IT FOR THE BANK?

Life is Better When the Bank is Onside

It is no secret that our standard of living in Canada has been dropping year by year for some time now.

The financial erosion we are experiencing has evolved in part because of the arrogance, debt, mismanagement, waste and corruption of the past few governments we have elected.

The largest contributor to this decline is the increasing cost of living in Canada, led by the high cost of taxation. With tax freedom day now arriving in Canada at the end of June, and with the cost of housing running at 25% to 30%, many families are feeling squeezed. These same families have a limited ability to increase their income or reduce their expenses. The Smith Manoeuvre can be a very large help because it reduces taxation and provides the means to build an investment portfolio which can provide a supplementary family income.

The Smith Manoeuvre, being a debt conversion strategy, requires the assistance of the financial institutions to allow us to reorganize and plan our debt. Any mortgage conversion strategy that is going to be good for your financial well being will have to benefit the powerful banks as well, or you can bet it won't be happening. The Smith

Manoeuvre will make even more money for the banks, right from the get-go, so they won't mind co-operating with you when you approach them to help you set it up.

The Smith Manoeuvre can be established for you at your current bank that holds your first mortgage, or at most any other bank or credit union. Other than the convenience of perhaps having all your banking at one facility, it will make little difference to you personally. If you have time and patience, you might shop around to find out which institution really wants your business enough to give you some perks for bringing The Smith Manoeuvre to them. Use a mortgage broker and a financial planner and let them find the best services for you, at the best price.

Way Back Then

When I was first attempting to interest a bank to support my invention in 1984, I was turned down by the Royal, the Montreal and the Bank of BC in that order. "Irregular" was the common reason given for refusing to participate to bring tax relief to Canadian mortgage holders.

Not one to give up, I decided I needed to talk to a bank president. Guessing that I would not be getting an audience any time soon with the president of the Royal Bank, I elected instead to talk to the head of VanCity Savings. The Chief Executive Officer was Larry Bell, recently arrived from his tenure as Deputy Minister of Finance for British Columbia. The VanCity board had decided they wanted to make things happen, and they couldn't have picked a better man for the job. I didn't know Larry Bell from a stick, but when I placed my call, the operator put me through without asking my name, and Larry Bell answered the phone himself. I liked him immediately. I told him I had an idea that would bring VanCity new customers at the expense of the big banks and he invited me in immediately for a chat.

Larry listened intently to my story, watched me draw my little pictorial, and when I was finished, he asked, "why isn't every Canadian doing this?" And a friendship was born.

Larry had his managers, corporate lawyers and senior staff review my proposal for comment. He took it to the board for their blessing, and within two months I began making mortgages deductible for the families in my client base. Larry Bell went on to be chairman of BC Hydro.

Larry was a finance MA, not a banker, and some would say that is the only reason he would even consider giving me and my Manoeuvre a chance. I think that is part of it, but I also think it is because he is a gentleman, and a gentle man, who saw potential where others didn't. What Larry allowed me to do for my clients, he is now doing for you because without his foresight and his intuition, I would probably not be writing this book for you today.

VanCity has grown to be the largest credit union in Canada. I am told that in the entire world, only the Boeing Credit Union is larger. VanCity continues to win prizes as one of the best companies to work for in Canada. It is home to Tom Hancock, the best banker I ever met. Tom was the branch manager of the North Vancouver branch of VanCity when we got The Smith Manoeuvre under way back in 1984. Tom is still with VanCity, and if you're lucky enough to live in B.C.'s Lower Mainland, you don't need to read this book any further. Just call Tom at (604) 877-7180. You can also call Diana Lingholt, the other best banker I ever met, (604)

877-7161. Diana knows The Smith Manoeuvre inside out. VanCity's Victoria expert is Bev Collison, 250-519-7424.

What was it that interested Larry Bell?

There are several reasons that Larry Bell was interested in The Smith Manoeuvre for VanCity's benefit.

1. Client profile

My client profile included presidents, managers, business people and lots of ordinary people too. At that time, having come from servicing largely the blue-collar sector, it was interesting to VanCity that they could perhaps attract other sectors too.

2. New customers

Since everybody already has a banking relationship, it is a market that is nearly 100% saturated. You may not feel sorry for your bank manager, but he is measured on how many new customers he signs up in the branch each year. As in most businesses, they need new business to grow, but that's tough to do in the banking business. By co-operating with me, the credit union attracted customers from other banks, other trust companies and other credit unions who were not offering The Smith Manoeuvre.

The bulk of my client base became VanCity customers. Why wouldn't they? VanCity allowed them to make their mortgage tax deductible, and their bank did not.

3.   Good customers

By virtue of the nature of the loan set-up I was proposing, Larry could see that his loan risk was very modest.   This was partly because his security for the investment lending would be the house, not the investments the client would be purchasing.   I am sure Larry was very confident that you would make fantastic investments with the money he was going to be lending you, but just in case, he would rather have your house as security for his loan to you. You are indifferent because you have already given your house as collateral to the Royal Bank, say, where you have your first mortgage.   Does it matter to you if the two banks are willing to share the same collateral security for their respective loans?

The main reason the loan risk was low was because Larry would not be lending to my client unless my client had first reduced the debt on his first mortgage.   Accordingly, Larry's lending was not increasing the customer's debt; it was simply keeping it at the same level.   Down goes the mortgage at the Royal; up goes the investment loan at VanCity.

Assuming that Larry would not accept my client if he did not have a good payment record on his existing first mortgage at the Royal, it would be a fairly safe bet that my client would not default at VanCity.   In other words, the Royal has already spent the time and money to qualify the customer for a mortgage, which reduces the risk to VanCity.

And to this day, no client on The Smith Manoeuvre has ever defaulted.   It is a fact that in all the years since 1984 that The Smith Manoeuvre has been operated by VanCity or any other credit union, not one mortgage loan, nor one investment loan has gone bad. It is also a fact that no bank or credit union that has utilized The Smith Manoeuvre has ever lost a penny of interest or principal to any client of mine. The Smith Manoeuvre business has been gold plated for VanCity and Coast Capital. You will know that all banks and credit unions expect and plan to have some mortgages and loans that fail, so it is a strong testament to The Smith Manoeuvre that the record is pristine.

4.   Collateral business

The new VanCity customer represented by my client seeking support to do The Smith Manoeuvre was bringing new lending business for VanCity. My proposal was that VanCity lend to my client every dollar that my client paid off against his first mortgage at the Royal. The security for this new loan for investment purposes would be the same house that was security for the first mortgage at the Royal.

In addition to their regular first mortgage payments at the Royal, my clients to make additional reductions against their first mortgage. VanCity would then lend back the amount that had been paid down on the first, and the new borrowings at VanCity would buy investments, thus the interest would be tax deductible. The faster my clients reduced their first mortgage, the faster they were able to borrow back the same amount, to be invested. The tax deductions got larger. They were applied against the first mortgage too, as additional pay downs. As soon as the first mortgage dropped, VanCity lent it back to my client again, and around we would go again. The first mortgage melted away, the investment loan at VanCity grew at exactly the same speed, no faster. More tax deductions, more first mortgage reductions, more borrowing from VanCity to invest, more tax deductions.

There is a giant sucking sound as VanCity starts to pull the 25-year asset, your mortgage, from the safe at the Royal Bank and puts it into the VanCity vault. The little guy has swiped the Royal's asset before they even know it has gone. Suddenly the asset has disappeared, an exceedingly troubling development because mortgage lending is a huge profit centre to the banks.

It's true that VanCity will be charging you interest as well. But there is a huge and fantastic difference. *The interest you pay at VanCity is tax deductible.* It never was deductible at the Royal. In addition to that, in making the conversion from non-deductible to deductible debt, you have built a large investment portfolio. Best of all, the investments are free and clear. No margin calls. VanCity did not take your investments as collateral because you gave VanCity the security of the same house that you had given the Royal. The Royal won't be needing the collateral anymore because they don't have your mortgage debt anymore. Their asset has evaporated to the nether regions.

Remember, the mortgage loan is your liability, therefore the bank's asset. Mortgage assets are the bank's lifeblood. They need as many mortgages as they can find. By allowing you to implement The Smith Manoeuvre, VanCity has found a way to obtain new mortgage assets by stealing them away from the big banks in exchange for giving you some unique and original investment financing, at no cost to VanCity. Once you are their happy customer they will be in a position to offer you legal services, RRSP/RRIF services, mutual funds, securities, trust services and insurance services. You are an important asset to any bank or credit union that is lucky enough to call you their customer.

There are Other Benefits for the Lending Institution

5.   They don't have to pay for the benefit you receive.

The banks will be pleased, nay anxious, to show you how to profit through The Smith Manoeuvre. After all, it is the tax department that is giving you this extraordinary financial benefit, not the banks, so why wouldn't they be pleased to profit by showing you the way to engineer these free tax refunds?

6.   Low up-front cost to the banks.

Usually when the banks offer you incentives to switch your mortgage to them, they pay a stiff up-front price. 5% cash back, free appraisal, free legals, front-end interest rate discounts – these are expensive methods for the banks to utilize to convince you to switch. They do it because they need more and more new business in order to grow, just like any other business. That they will absorb these punishing up front costs in order to get you to place your mortgage with them is testament to the huge value the mortgage business represents to the lending institutions.

The banks will be delighted to provide you the new Smith Manoeuvre Mortgage because it will cost them very little to give you the financial arrangements required to put the strategy in place.

7.   The banks will sell you the investments you need to make the program work.

Because my strategy does not work if you don't borrow funds to invest (in order to bring in new money via tax deductions) you will find yourself borrowing to invest. This is fine for you because it makes the program work and you will be grateful to have an investment portfolio that grows rapidly to provide your personal pension plan.

The banks, however, have also gotten into the investment business. They will wish to facilitate The Smith Manoeuvre for you because their costs to do so are light, and because the benefits you receive are at the expense of the tax department. They will also want to sell you the investments you need to buy in order to get the tax deductions. This may well be the biggest of all the advantages for the lending institutions – they get first crack at selling investments to the family to whom they just did the favour of rearranging their financing so that the family could implement The Smith Manoeuvre. What a lovely business position to be in.

The minute this book is on the shelves, if I were a bank, I would be working 25 hours a day to ensure that when you walk in to ask that The Smith Manoeuvre be set up for you, I will be ready to supply your investments as well as your financing.

What will your revised bank statement look like?

It's really very simple to do. As your banker, I would offer you a monthly bank statement that showed how much your first mortgage went down in the last 30 days whether by regular mortgage payments or over payments. On the same page I would show you that the exact amount of the mortgage reduction had been loaned back to you to buy the three or six mutual funds that you chose when you signed up for The Smith Manoeuvre.

Your statement would show:

a. how much your mortgage dropped that month
b. that the same amount was loaned back to you the same day from a separate creditline (tracking is important)
c. which investments were purchased with the borrowed money
d. how much interest was charged on the investment loan so that you can see how much your tax deduction increased that month
e. your total deductible interest accumulated year to date
f. what the total value of your investments were standing at from inception to date. This investment pool is free and clear because your house is the security for the borrowings, not the investments.

Your financial planner will help you choose a financial institution that will offer the services you need to optimize your tax deductions using The Smith Manoeuvre.

8. Self maintaining asset base

It was Larry Bell who pointed out to me one of the most important benefits he could see accruing to VanCity.

All banks have a built in problem with their mortgage loan assets. The day you made your first mortgage payment, you reduced your principal a tiny amount, in addition to paying a huge amount of non-deductible interest to the bank. While you feel good about paying down your mortgage balance, the bank feels bad, because you have reduced their asset. They start immediately to find other people who need mortgages in order to replace the assets lost each day due to mortgage payments being made across Canada.

It was Larry who realized that because my clients would be re-borrowing to invest at the same speed as they were paying off the first mortgage, the consequence would be that his bank's asset, your debt, would be maintained at the same level. Why would you pay off a loan you had just made deductible?

Why indeed! Your intent should be to die at age 130 still owing VanCity that same amount so that you can keep claiming the deductible interest every year until you die.

Assume that after a few years, the whole mortgage has been converted to the deductible interest investment loan. Assume you keep the deductible loan going, so that you would have the same tax deductions year after year.

These annual, repeating, large, free, no-cost, gratis and non-taxable annual tax refunds would be pooled with the former first mortgage payment which you don't need to make anymore because the conversion is complete.

In practice, you would reduce your newly converted investment loan with the total of the tax refunds and the former first mortgage payment, but just for a day. The rule is that if you reduce your creditline, you can borrow the money back, less the interest expense (tax-deductible) for that month. You would borrow back the difference and invest it. You would continue each month to build your investment portfolio at the maximum rate, the tax deductions would be maximum, and the deductible loan would stay constantly level as you paid interest only, on the loan. The interest expense would continue to be deductible every year for the rest of your life and your investment portfolio would continue to grow as you added more capital each month. If your income was a bit low when you retired, you might slow down or cease to add capital into your investment portfolio. If it were still too low, perhaps you would set up a SWP, or Systematic Withdrawal Plan such that the investment portfolio started sending you a cheque each month, for a change.

If you complete the conversion, and wish to have no debt at all, good or bad, you could elect to divert tax refunds plus former first mortgage payments to reduce the deductible loan. The price of no debt would be tax deductions that would get smaller each year as the deductible loan was reduced. As well, if your excess cash flow is being diverted to pay off this good loan, by definition, your excess cash flow is not building a larger investment portfolio, to the detriment of your retirement planning.

The point is that you will have a choice between continuing your investment program or paying off your new tax-deductible loan. This is a luxury many Canadians will not enjoy if they do not avail themselves of at least employing The Smith Manoeuvre to convert the debt from the bad kind to the good kind. Convert your debt to the good kind, and then decide whether to keep it or pay it off.

That is the very least even the most debt-adverse citizen should entertain. If you already have the debt of a first mortgage, at least convert it from bad debt to good debt. The benefits are large:

1. It costs you nothing but for the appraisal and the cost of the mortgage documents, which many lending institutions will absorb if you simply ask, (they need mortgage business with low risk customers and it costs them very little both to verify the value of your house and to prepare a readvanceable mortgage using in-house or related specialists).

2. You will reduce your first mortgage with tax deductions that are free for the asking.

3. You will have an investment portfolio that will grow year after year contributing income into your retirement – an investment portfolio that, otherwise, you would not have had.

4. If your investment program is made up of financial assets such as mutual funds, stocks and bonds, you will have complete liquidity if for any reason you need to reverse the program.

You will be pleased when you decide to utilize The Smith Manoeuvre. The financial institutions will also be glad of your decision. But will the tax department be glad you did? Will the Minister of Revenue be excited in a pleasant and positive way when you have engineered all these continuous and very large tax deductions year after year after year? Hmmm-mm.

Just who is providing all this new money you are getting from all these new tax deductions you are claiming for your new found deductible interest?

9

WHAT'S IN IT FOR CANADA?

The Tax Department, the Government and the Country

There is a rumour that the tax department is planning a new tax return for Canadians. They have been listening to citizens who think its format should be a simpler form, and this is the first draft:

1. How much did you make last year?
2. Send it in.

Who Pays?

Just where is all this new money coming from that your family is going to receive in order for you to utilize The Smith Manoeuvre, *so that you can*:

1. reduce your first mortgage, *so that you can*
2. borrow back your new found equity the same day, *so that you can*
3. buy new investments with the new, borrowed money, *so that you can*
4. generate deductible investment-loan interest expense, *so that you can*

5. claim tax deductions, *so that you can*
6. get free tax refund cheques, *so that you can*
7. reduce your first mortgage, *so that you can*
8. borrow back,........etc., etc.

It becomes apparent that *the tax department is the entity that is going to provide the new money for your family* when you engage The Smith Manoeuvre. There are many articles and books written that show you how to pay your mortgage off faster, and this is good because it means you will pay less interest to the bank over the life of the mortgage.

But it is important to understand that these strategies, such as switching from monthly mortgage payments to making payments every two weeks, are only effective because you are putting *more of your own money* against the mortgage sooner. It is the "sooner" part that shortens the life of the mortgage, thus reducing the total amount of interest that you will pay. While that's good, it is still *your money* that is being *spent sooner*. The payoff for you comes at the back end of the mortgage, which is many years off. Would you be interested in having your payoff start right now?

The Smith Manoeuvre is quite different because it is the only mortgage strategy that generates a new and incremental income for your family via tax deductions, which you are then able to use to pay down your mortgage faster than otherwise possible. In addition, you will have a pool of assets you have purchased with the money you borrowed to invest - all because you receive new cash for your family as a result of tax refund cheques that you receive from the tax department. This should make you feel better towards the tax department.

Because this investment strategy converts the traditionally non-deductible interest of a house mortgage loan into deductible investment-loan interest, the tax department will not be receiving as much tax from you as they have become accustomed to receiving. They will still be collecting a lot from you, but less than usual.

In the narrow confines of the office of the Minister of Revenue, there might be some early consternation at the initial drop in tax revenue because of the refund cheques he will be writing to you when you start using The Smith Manoeuvre. Fortunately, the Minister of Revenue, in the longer term, is quite happy to have you using The Smith Manoeuvre. The other cabinet ministers are happy about it too.

Deductible Interest – the Lubricant of Business Investment

Most industrialized nations allow the interest expense on business loans to be deducted from the business income of the corporation that does the borrowing. This act reduces the income tax bill of the company. The government understands quite well that it is in their own best interest to provide the tax incentive of tax-deductible interest to businesses making investment decisions for the benefit of their own company. For instance, if the loan interest is deductible, then it makes more palatable the decision to build plant and infrastructure.

The taxman knows that if he does his part to make it easier for the companies to make decisions to borrow to invest in infrastructure, research, marketing and such, there will likely be more profits in the future for the company which the taxman will be able to tax. In addition, the growth of the company will require growth in the number of employed people who the tax department will be only too happy to tax to the max.

This also reduces the number of people on the welfare rolls, reducing government expense in that important area. The people who are working ostensibly spend more providing a stimulus to the economy, further increasing the flows of cash which government also gets to tax to death. You are familiar with the GST, no doubt.

And finally, whereas people who are without work are a drain on the system on a current basis, they are also not investors in RRSP's and other investments, which would provide future income for their retirement. The government gains in a large way if the population is employed. These are some of the reasons that the tax department is happy to allow deductible interest for businesses that borrow to increase their business. And so it should be.

Personal Investing and Tax Deductible Interest

The wealthier of the population, after the expenses we all have for food, clothing, shelter and income tax, have some money left over at the end of the month to invest. They are also able to afford expensive lawyers and accountants to show them how to take out bank loans for investment purposes and then to deduct their interest on their investment loans, simultaneously. Invest and also reduce income tax at the same time? That's fine by the tax department, and is in fact encouraged by the tax department. All wealthy people have done this, are doing it or will do it.

Because the wealthy are able and willing to invest to improve their economic position to even higher levels, they provide the rest of us a service of great benefit. Because of their investment money, new businesses are funded, and the new businesses hire new people. The businesses and the people are taxed, so the taxman is grateful enough to the investor that the taxman will allow the wealthy investor to deduct the interest on any loan he takes out for the purpose of earning more income. The rationale is the same as it is for the first example of the taxman allowing deductions of interest expense for companies.

The 90% or more of the population that are not classified as wealthy are not usually investors. It is not because they don't want to be, it's because they usually find that the cash runs out before the month runs out. How could anyone justify using cash to invest for say a 10% return when they are carrying credit card debt at 19%? We know that only 2 in 3 Canadians can afford to invest in an RRSP even with its great benefits such as tax deductibility of the principal investment plus tax-free compounding. Small wonder that by far the bulk of Canadians will come up short of cash flow when the pay cheque stops at retirement day.

The Smith Manoeuvre works for all Canadians who have a mortgage, whether they are wealthy or not. There is a huge pool of mortgage payers in Canada that are not in the wealthy category. They are working hard to make ends meet, they are getting an education, and they are raising kids. They are also finding it tough to get through many months without employing the credit card.

The tax department will be delighted to find out that The Smith Manoeuvre is going to turn this huge group of taxpayers into investors. More investors in Canada means more businesses funded with new funds as the mortgages are converted from dead-end home mortgages into investment loans.

The benefits for Canada will be the same as they are from companies that invest, and from wealthy Canadians that invest. And therefore, in the same way the tax department is happy to allow deductions for interest on loans to make income when it applies to business and wealthy investors, they will be happy to allow it for the not wealthy. If you are in the not-wealthy category, the tax department is standing by to start sending you tax refund cheques if you are wise enough to convert your bad debt to good debt.

Because of the resultant new cash that will begin arriving in the homes of legions of ordinary Canadians derived from these tax refund cheques, these families will be better off themselves. They will have pools of investments instead of dead-end house mortgages, and they will generate lower and lower taxes as they invest more and more. These families will be less likely to need government assistance during their working life or in their retirement.

The tax department is the apparent loser in the short term, but a winner in the longer term. This is why the government, in its wisdom, will bless The Smith Manoeuvre and the wealth it will bring to homeowners with mortgages, be they wealthy or not so wealthy.

Many years ago, Joe Clark was elected prime minister partly on the strength of his promise to give Canadians tax-deductible mortgages. To his credit, the law was changed and the tax return forms the following year did provide some partial deductions. The Liberals cancelled the program when Joe was defeated at the next election. The flaw in the program was that it was a giveaway. There was no requirement for the homeowner to do any investing/conversion of the mortgage to earn the deductions. You will receive no tax refunds from the taxman using The Smith Manoeuvre unless and until you convert your debt from bad to good. Investing is good for the people, and therefore it's good for Canada. In the final analysis, this is why the CRA will be happy to support The Smith Manoeuvre, and this is why you will receive free tax refunds.

It will sound to some like it is too good to be true, that life is a zero sum game and therefore it can't possibly be as represented. Classical and modern economists might not agree on the foregoing as it applies to theory. But if you believe in free enterprise and the goodness of capitalism-with-caring, you will understand that we can all be beneficiaries if we enable and encourage this program. The Smith Manoeuvre simply extends tax and investment benefits that have always been in place for business and the wealthy, to the less wealthy in our society. Surely that will be good for all of us.

10

SUMMARY

You have learned about The Smith Manoeuvre, which is a combination of several different strategies available to you that, once implemented, will improve the financial well being of your family in dramatic fashion, with very little cost.

These strategies rapidly convert bad debt (non-deductible) to good debt (tax deductible) and they work on any current or future non-deductible interest debt you may have, including house mortgages, car loans and consolidation loans.

The Smith Manoeuvre *does not require* that you increase your debt. Instead you will simply arrange to keep the amount of your existing debt constant for the interval of time it takes to *convert* the debt you have now, from the bad kind to the good kind. Because debt is not increasing, this is not classified as a leveraging program. It is a debt conversion strategy.

When the conversion process has been completed, you may choose to resume eliminating your debt, even though it is good debt (the interest expense is tax deductible and will be providing you free tax refund cheques).

In the alternative, you may decide that you wish to leave the loan in place, paying deductible interest only. In this case you will continue to receive tax refund cheques for the rest of your life, and instead of reducing the loan with your cash flow, you could choose to continue to buy investments for the rest of your life as well. This is typically what wealthy people do as there is no doubt that the growth of net worth is far superior in this latter case. But some will insist on zero debt no matter what it costs to attain it. The decision is yours to make, at your pleasure.

The length of time it will take to convert your existing bad debt to good debt is influenced by several factors. These include your family cash flow, the amount of deductible interest you can claim to get tax refunds, and the value of assets you currently own. These assets might better be liquidated to provide more cash to reduce your non-deductible loans such as your house mortgage. In addition, the efficiency of The Smith Manoeuvre can be dramatically improved by diverting existing monthly savings and investment plans against the non-deductible debt. Persons who operate unincorporated businesses or who wish to utilize leveraging strategies can multiply the value of The Smith Manoeuvre in dramatic fashion.

As the non-deductible loans are reduced by the foregoing strategies, the identical amount of money is re-borrowed from the same or a different bank to purchase replacement assets. These assets will be free and clear because the security for the borrowing will be the house, just as the house was the security for the original non-deductible mortgage loan.

Because these new assets are free and clear, there can be no margin calls. If your family were subsequently subjected to a financial disaster, such that your house was in danger, you would obviously sell off some of your free and clear assets to ensure you kept your home. The process is reversible.

The Smith Manoeuvre relies on the tax department rules that money borrowed to buy your home, cars, vacations and consolidation, does not generate deductible interest. On the other hand, when you borrow money with the expectation of earning more income, the interest expense of that loan *will* be a tax deduction. It is the kind of debt you have that determines its deductibility.

You have the debt already. It is bad debt because its interest expense is not tax deductible. You might as well get it converted to the good kind of debt – deductible debt. You will enjoy receiving those tax refund cheques. They are free and there is no tax on the proceeds. The conversion from bad debt to good debt is effected by your purchase of new investments of your choice, one more very large benefit of The Smith Manoeuvre for your family.

The Smith Manoeuvre is a legal strategy utilizing standard Canada Revenue Agency tax rules. It is available to any Canadian family with 25% or more equity in their home, or with the ability to engineer 25% or more equity by paying down or borrowing enough to reach that level. Borrowing from Peter to pay Paul is not always a bad thing to do. Some financial institutions will allow The Smith Manoeuvre to be set up with less than 25%, but there are incremental costs for the high ratio mortgage insurance.

The Smith Manoeuvre utilizes strategies routinely practised by businesses and wealthy individuals with the assistance of expensive lawyers and accountants. Finally, via The Smith Manoeuvre, ordinary Canadians with ordinary incomes will be able to enjoy these strategies previously available only to the wealthy.

To enable you to calculate your personal outcomes if you were to employ The Smith Manoeuvre for your family, you will want to order The Smithman Calculator at *www.smithman.net*, or photocopy the order form on the last page of this book to send in. This versatile software will show you the results arising from any partial or complete implementation of the program. It will allow you to compare "what-if" strategies such as interest rate variations or amortization alterations.

The financial course currently being travelled by most Canadians these days will yield poor results and broken dreams. Many Canadians are headed for a reverse mortgage unless they change their strategy of "first get rid of the mortgage, and then start to build on investment portfolio." Adopting The Smith Manoeuvre will dramatically improve your chances of optimizing your ability to build significantly more family net worth than you presumed possible. If you implement The Smith Manoeuvre, the likelihood that you will be forced into a reverse mortgage in your retirement is miniscule.

While it is possible for a person with some financial experience to put The Smith Manoeuvre into practice, I recommend you employ a financial planner to do this work for you. A full service financial planner will be able to tailor your financial situation to your best personal advantage. There are also other circumstances and linkages that a good financial planner will accommodate on your behalf to ensure no opportunity is missed to optimize the results for your family. Go to my website *www.smithman.net* to get assistance in locating a financial planner in your part of Canada, who is qualified to assist you with implementation of The Smith Manoeuvre.

Factors that influence the financial well being of your family have not been encouraging in Canada in the past few years, and a turn around may be slower coming than we would hope. This means we will have to depend less on government, and more on our own resources. The Smith Manoeuvre is remarkably efficient at raising large amounts of real, new wealth for your family while it generates welcome and free tax refunds. As well, it causes us to immediately begin building that all-important investment portfolio that will give us peace of mind as it builds, free and clear. It is a comfort to live your life knowing you have liquid assets to call upon if the need ever arises.

So join the hundreds of Canadians who are already in the process of converting their bad debt to good debt, or who have completed the process. You too can enjoy these financial gains for the benefit of your family.

I

APPENDICES

EXPERIENCED FINANCIAL PLANNERS

Unless you have financial planning experience, I recommend you locate a financial planner in your area that is interested in assisting with the implementation of *The Smith Manoeuvre* for you. A few minutes on the telephone to find someone who is willing to help will be very worthwhile.

On the website www.smithman.net is a tab called "Find A Planner" where we are listing financial planners who are willing to assist with The Smith Manoeuvre, usually for a fee. Most will be happy to make your first meeting complimentary, but do inquire.

If you are a financial planner, and if you would be willing to assist mortgage owners with this strategy, please submit your request via my website after clicking on "Find a Planner" on our home page. There are a few free marketing tools for your use. There is no charge for this service, but for the benefit of all, the listed planners and customers, I do require that you be licensed and a member of a regulated professional body, so please bear with us when we review your request.

Appendix B

BRIAN DOUGHERTY LTD.
CHARTERED ACCOUNTANTS

202 - 315 WEST 1st STREET
NORTH VANCOUVER, B.C. V7M 1B5
TELEPHONE: (604) 986-7307
FAX: (604) 984-6919
E-MAIL: brian@briandougherty.com

June 24, 2002

Smith Consulting Group Ltd.
104 – 7851 East Saanich Road
Saanichton, BC
V8M 2B4

Dear Sirs:

Re: Review of Excel Model Titled The Smith Manoeuvre

We have conducted a review of the Excel spreadsheet entitled The Smith Manoeuvre version Model 6 with a view to confirming it's basic mathematical assumptions, mechanics of operation and subsequent results.

Amortization results using Model 6 with several different variables as to rates and amortization periods were compared against Mortgage 2 Pro for Windows software, version 4.05.004, and the results were precisely the same in all tests we preformed.   The interest compounding variables of Model 6 are limited to two interest compounding methodologies, standard Canadian mortgage compounding which is twice yearly, not in advance, and standard monthly compounding which covers American mortgages and standard loan amortization in both countries.

...2

Model 6 includes a standard amortization calculator as well as a modified amortization calculator which allows the user to quickly compare the effects of making additional payments against mortgages and loans in order to reduce the total interest expense of those mortgages and loans. In addition to the foregoing, Model 6 supplies additional capability to extrapolate the conversion of the interest saved into additional investments over the same periods of time represented by the original amortization expectations of the original loan.

The net result is that Model 6 is able to show the favourable effect of converting the non-deductible interest of the house mortgage into the deductible interest of an equivalent investment loan which in turn, generates tax refunds for the user.

We have checked the assumptions and mechanics of these sections of Model 6 and we confirm that the assumptions are acceptable and the calculated results are as would be expected.

Yours very truly,

Brian Dougherty Ltd.
Chartered Accountants

Per: Brian Dougherty

/blc

II

LINKS

Websites

The Smith Manoeuvre | _www.smithman.net_
Canadian Assoc. of Financial Planners | _www.cafp.org_
Garth Turner | _www.garth.ca_
The Fraser Institute | _www.fraserinstitute.ca_
Andex Charts | _www.andexcharts.com_
Talbot Stevens | _www.talbotstevens.com_
Manulife | _www.manulifeone.com_
Canadian Taxpayers Federation | _www.taxpayer.com_
National Citizens Coalition | _www.morefreedom.org_
VanCity Savings Credit Union | _www.vancity.com_
Coast Capital Savings | _www.coastcapitalsavings.com_
Amortization.com | _www.morgij2.com_

III

WHAT PEOPLE ARE SAYING...

"*The Smith Manoeuvre* is an ESSENTIAL element to building wealth and should be used by all who have a 'non-deductible interest mortgage"

Michel McMahon, B.Comm.

"Just wanted to thank Mr. Smith for caring enough to write such a significant book. I will definitely be implementing his system ASAP. An appreciative mortgage/home owner."

Rohan Wallen

"I'll keep this short by saying thank you very much for your lifetime achievement of producing a very useful book and sharing it with the public. It has helped my clients tremendously and has created wealth in my own situation as well."

Andre Cyr, Montreal, Quebec

"I first got introduced to the Smith Manoeuvre when a friend mentioned your book to me. I have since read it and found it quite interesting. Being a financial planner, when I first started to read the book I thought there wasn't much new in this UNTIL I got to the part about arranging the mortgage financing. I hadn't heard of any banks arranging this sort of a wrap around, re-advanceable mortgage the way it is described in the book. Innovative!"

Ray Schwalme, CFP, BA York Financial Group

"Loved your book! Absolutely fabulous! I ordered a copy of your book last week and I read it cover to cover in two evenings. As a former financial planner, I had a sense very early into your book that this would be a life changing experience for me. I have already called my bank about putting your "manoeuvre" into action."

Tony Richardson,
Project Manager AdvisorNet Communications Inc.

"The book is an excellent example of integrating opportunities in a new way to everyone's benefit and I appreciate the fact that it takes advantage of no one. It will be beneficial to the country as more homeowners use *The Smith Manoeuvre.*"

Tom Sutton, Vancouver, B.C.

"I read your book, *The Smith Manoeuvre,* on the train from Toronto to Ottawa last night. Even though I had had an 18-hour day, the concepts you shared were so powerful that I couldn't sleep last night! Since then, I've potentially two new clients after only a five minute conversation with each of them."

Karl Ruban, B.Comm. (Hons), CA, CMA, CFP, RFP,
Toronto, Ontario

"Dear Fraser ... Three months ago I purchased your book about the Smith Manoeuvre. It's excellent! Last night my wife and I took your advice and had our first meeting with our new financial advisor, Karl Ruban, whose name I found on your website. The meeting went well beyond what we had anticipated both in terms of the amount of time we spent together, and the amount of information and help that was provided. As a result, my wife and I are completely reorganizing our financial affairs with Karl's expert assistance. If we follow his advice, Karl says that we should be able to implement the Smith Manoeuvre in about two years. I very much look forward to that day and wish to thank you, Fraser, in particular, for bringing enlightenment to our lives, and for making me feel for the first time in my life that I am taking the right road to financial health."

Dal Corran, Toronto, Ontario

"As Leader of the Reform Party and a founder of the Canadian Alliance, one of my greatest concerns has been the excessively high taxes paid by Canadians. While tax relief through tax reform is urgently needed and will eventually come, the strategy proposed by Fraser Smith offers every Canadian who has a mortgage the possibility of significant tax relief right now. I would encourage you to read Fraser's book and discuss his strategy with your banker or financial planner as soon as possible."

Preston Manning,
Former Leader of the Official Opposition.

"I'm so excited about going through my client base and applying your strategy and getting new clients by doing the same. I've been helping people convert non-deductible debt to deductible debt since I entered the business in 1995. I have never had people borrow to pay their deductible interest, which, has created cash flow issues and prevented many from participating. I had to read the Income Tax Act for my own peace of mind. The section about deducting interest on interest is actually found in 20(1)(d) which refers to the interest deduction found in 20(c). If anyone else feels the need to read this like I did, they can find it at here."http://laws.justice.gc.ca/en/I-3.3/64401.html

David Dagley, CFP

"Smith argues in the language of revolutionaries (albeit financial planning revolutionaries) that he's offering members of the Canadian middle class a way to achieve financial emancipation, allowing "the mass population to use tools usually available only to the richest 5 per cent of the population."

Jeff Sanford,
IE Money
Manoeuvre Money From Your House

"...a snowballing virtuous circle that lets you tweak the noses of both the banks and the taxman."

Jonathan Chevreau, National Post

"I have three of the original 10 books left and I have three mortgages set up so far. I'm really having fun with this program ... Accountants love it .... the clients save money ... ya gotta love it. "

Lloyd Snyder, CFP, PFP, BA
Charlottetown, PEI

"Mr. Novak: I recently discovered this wonderful gem of a book which I am sure you are familiar with, *The Smith Manoeuvre* by Fraser Smith. After only reading two thirds of the book, I am so excited to start the program.... I am contemplating taking a trip to Kelowna just for a consultation with you, to determine if my family and I are in a position to take advantage of the "Smith Manoeuvre" plan, and get help with implementing as much of the plan as financially possible."

Eric Groom,
Airdrie, Alberta

"I would like to tell you that I introduced your strategy to my financial planner and he was very excited about it. He said he'd start to offer this strategy to other clients. Again thank you for the great idea."

Mark Libant,
Ottawa, Ont.

"I am halfway through your book, but haven't been able to finish it, for two reasons. One, I can't read it during the day because I have two small sons at home who keep me very busy, and two, I can't read it at night because I get too excited reading about all these great ideas, that I can't go to sleep."

Daphne Stuart,
Courtenay, BC

"Fraser Smith's door ought to have been knocked down hundreds of times. It ought to have been torn from its hinges and thrust aside as mortgage-weary Canadians stormed in to see the man who could help them pay down that mortgage faster and write off the interest like their American cousins."

"Financial Planner Manoeuvres Rules and Banks to Your Benefit"
Andrew Duffy,
Times Colonist

"You're converting mortgage interest into a 100-per-cent tax deduction, year after year, which will garner you nice fat tax refunds."

B.C. Business "Home Leverage"

"Really simple. Really lovely. And legal several times over, thanks to RevCan, which has tested the deductibility of investment interest several times and, in November [2001], lost in the Supreme Court of Canada.

Fraser, with the help of the bankers at VanCity Credit Union (the second-largest credit union in the world), has been engineering this feat for all kinds of people for years, from chefs and hostesses, to school principals and corporate presidents. His just-published book is clean, spare and witty."

"Borrow Your Way to Tax Freedom",
Elizabeth Nickson, National Post

"Ms. Nickson ... Your column [Borrow your way to Tax Freedom] was the newspaper equivalent of clouds lifting after about 7 months of overcast skies...I am 37 years old, married with 2 young kids... My wife is a stay @ home mom, who works part-time one day per week.

I am probably earning double what I originally did 10 years ago, but I might as well paint a picture of a sitting duck on my front, a bull's-eye on my back, grab a megaphone and yell "TAX ME" inside the RevCan office.

I am going to arrange to meet with a financial advisor next week and get the ball rolling on this. I'll let you know how it works out. You certainly did me and thousands of other Canadian readers a big favour today, by offering a glimmer of hope. The best way control the beast that is government is simply not to feed it."

James, Whitby , Ontario Taxpayer

"A must read for those looking to reduce their tax bill and increase their financial security."

Canadian Taxpayers Federation The Taxpayer

"The mortgage you designed is incredible and a benefit to everyone, and the simplicity of the explanation is excellent.

The real trick is the painless investing of capital through the specialized mortgage. In this respect it is both a tax technique and a simple savings and investing program.

All in all, "wonderful," as it brings a simple plan to ordinary people. The mortgage industry should give you a medal; however the bulk will still be slow because of ingrained histories."

C. (Cliff) H. Fryers, B.Comm., LL.B.
Chairman & CEO
WhiteIron Inc.

"My sincerest thanks to you for sharing the wisdom contained in your magnificent book "The Smith Manoeuvre".

I completed the reading this morning and was impressed with your very clear, concise and exacting explanation of the leverage and the many advantages, in using 'good' debt to enhance one's net worth."

Although my mortgage is only in the $85,000 range and the fact that I am rapidly approaching the senior- citizen category, I want to take advantage of your strategy, if for no other reason than the pocket books of my kids, when I die at the ripe age of 130. Please accept my thanks for sharing such vital and sensible information."

Tony Quarless,
Retired CEO,
Victoria Real Estate Board

"Great book and great software.... and thanks for the technical support... worked like a charm."

Steve Hodges
Hull, Quebec

"Any time we make a mortgage payment - say it's a 5% mortgage - most of us have to remember, we're earning 10%, giving half of it away in tax to leave ourselves with that 5% worth in the mortgage. Having it tax deductible is just a huge differentiation in the calibre of debt you've got."

Michael Campbell,
Host of MoneyTalks
CKNW Interview

"Smith deserves credit for introducing debt-conversion strategies to a wider audience."

"Book promises to liberate the little guy"
Michael Kane, Vancouver Sun

"Smith outlines the techniques for making a mortgage tax deductible in Canada, complete with an endorsement from Preston Manning."

Prince George Free Press

"Too many Canadians are delaying their investment program until it is too late. His [Smith's] answer is to turn bad debt into good debt - in other words, converting the largest debt of a person's lifetime - their mortgage - into a means of literally, having their cake and eating it too."

Peninsula News Review
"Try the Smith Manoeuvre on your mortgage"

"I felt it was propitious that Fraser Smith had targeted VanCity to champion his unique financial strategy for mortgage holders in Canada. The Smith Manoeuvre, as it became to be known, was simple and elegant. We attracted many new customers over the years by virtue of our support of the program.

My question back then still stands today - "Why isn't every Canadian making his mortgage tax deductible?" Perhaps the publishing of The Smith Manoeuvre will make it happen."

Larry Bell,
Former CEO,
VanCity

"As a columnist, author, tax paying citizen with a house mortgage, I may not be your "average" Canadian. I do know that my future is significantly brighter since I implemented *The Smith Manoeuvre* to convert my interest expense into tax deductions.

In addition to my new, free tax deduction refund cheques which I have received for two years now, *The Smith Manoeuvre* has allowed me to start building an investment portfolio that otherwise was going to have to wait until my mortgage was paid off. Sooner is better. Much better."

Elizabeth Nickson, MBA,
National Post Columnist

"Loved your book - a few twists to the 'debt-swap' I've been implementing for years. What a simple and sensible strategy for the everyday Canadian."

Stefano Francescut, CFP
Branch Manager, Investment Planning Counsel of Canada